JUSTICE
REVEALED

JUSTICE REVEALED

A COP DISCOVERS GOD'S IMPARTIAL FAIRNESS

Jim McNeff

CROSSLINK
PUBLISHING

Justice Revealed: A Cop Discovers God's Impartial Fairness

CrossLink Publishing
www.crosslinkpublishing.com

ISBN 978-1-63357-070-2

Library of Congress Control Number: 2016933152

The evidence that God loves those serving in law enforcement, and that he is creating a revival in us, is that he gifted Jim McNeff to write and minister specifically to our areas of need. Jim conveys the love and truth of God's Word through stories that connect with the heart of cops. *Justice Revealed* is a versatile, powerfully practical resource.

– Jonathan Parker
Pastor, Cop Church Chattanooga
Founder, Covered Law Enforcement
National Board Member, Fellowship of Christian Peace Officers

Justice Revealed is thought provoking and causes you to step back and reflect. Jim's transparency will draw the reader to connect on what is physically seen and yet see the spiritual in ways unimaginable.

– Allison Uribe
Founder, Wives on Duty Ministries

I read *Justice Revealed* with my wife as a daily devotional. We really enjoyed getting to read Jim's thoughts, especially when illustrated by his past police experiences. He has a great way of connecting a suitable story to exemplify the right passage of Scripture!

– Jon Jobe, Community Pastor
Bent Tree Bible Fellowship

The way Jim has weaved police stories that resonate with LEO's like myself and the truth of Scripture is superb. He has shared the Gospel in a manner that is both entertaining and enlightening. Well done!

– Clyde Foreman
Regional Security Manager—Central US, Tesoro Corporation
Past Chief of Operations, Chelan County Sheriff, SAC—FBI

CONTENTS

Section Ten – Debriefing   161

42   God's 9-1-1 System   163
43   Tell Ophidia to Take a Hike   167
44   Gracious Redemption   173

x

INTRODUCTION

Spiritual warfare is rampant. Lucifer, the fallen angel who became Satan, is duplicitous in his tactics. *Justice Revealed* will engage in the battle. It is a series of instructive vignettes, illustrations, and allegories that combine my professional experience in criminal justice with a personal proclamation of God's impartial fairness—his perfect justice. Since many peace officers have a latent sense of humor, you will find some satire, parody, paradox, symbolism, and a soliloquy as well. Cops are typically thick-skinned, but secretly softhearted, so there is a prose or two for good measure.

The small bites of insight from each chapter are designed to take less time than it would require to connect during a coffee break. Plus the dialogue will be rich and meaningful as we journey between the laws of the land and the laws of God.

The statue of Lady Justice holds a balanced scale and wears a blindfold. She represents a criminal justice system that pursues accountability without regard to status or classification—favorable or unfavorable. The conduct of each person is to be weighed without preference or prejudice. But we all know it falls short. It is a good system that possesses the imperfections of humanity, because flawed people administer it.

While perfection is the goal in the criminal justice system, we acknowledge it cannot be achieved since blemished individuals manage the organizations that hold people accountable. Even wise and highly educated police commanders, prosecutors, defense counselors, judges, and jurists do not possess God's universally supreme overwatch capability. It is a trait that is humanly unattainable.

God's divine system of justice is ideal, and it's revealed to us in his Word, by the Holy Spirit, and in nature. It is not a mystery! God's justice not only allows but also chooses deficient people and transforms them to practitioners of holiness. Once they have been obedient to God's call in their life, they have been sealed with the perfect qualifications made available through Jesus.

The criminal justice system began simply, but has become more complicated by layers of codification and case law. Humanly speaking, we've tried to perfect our effort, but there is no shortage of people who've been victimized by the system that is designed to be their advocate.

God's system of justice has been made confusing by people trying to figure out a sovereign Creator, but Jesus said it's as simple as coming to him like children. A cloud of witnesses throughout history surrounds us, and in the present day there are more that can testify to God's mercy and grace—and I am one!

The apostle Paul wrote a message to his protégé Timothy that fits nicely with the purpose propelling *Justice Revealed:*

> First of all, then, I urge that supplications, prayers, intercessions, and thanksgivings be made for all people, for kings and all who are in high positions, that we may lead a peaceful and quiet life, godly and dignified in every way. This is good, and it is pleasing in the sight of God our Savior, who desires all people to be saved and to come to the knowledge of the truth. For there is one God, and there is one mediator between God and

men, the man Christ Jesus, who gave himself as a ransom for all, which is the testimony given at the proper time (1 Timothy 2:1–6).

Now is the time. *Justice Revealed* will continue the testimony that began more than two thousand years ago. The gospel of Christ is for everyone, and the law enforcement perspective that I offer will provide a unique angle to a timeless treasure for all to experience.

"Are police officers one of the less-evangelized people groups in America?" asked Dr. Marvin Olasky, editor-in-chief of *WORLD Magazine*, when commenting on my first book, *The Spirit behind Badge 145.* "With life-or-death decisions to make, they certainly form one of the neediest," he continued, and I couldn't agree more. God has called me to evangelize and disciple, so this book is heavily flavored with these topics. Yet I will also capitalize on the acts of fellowship, worship, and ministry as we voyage through Scripture to discover and disclose God's perfect fairness—his *Justice Revealed.*

While I thrive on biblical instruction with significant depth, I also believe in the basic message of the gospel to alter behavior and indescribably change lives. I am convinced that solid teaching from the Bible is necessary to incrementally grow in faith. Yet no teacher or preacher can replace the penetrating effect of Scripture in the hearts and minds of people responding in faith to God's call on their life. I hope to pull you into the narrative with influencing stories and illustrations, but God's Word is present to seal the deal.

Just as Paul prayed for those he ministered to, I pray for each reader with earnest sincerity. May God make known his truth to you in *Justice Revealed.*

SECTION ONE
THE JUSTICE SYSTEM

WORDS THAT WOUND

1

*"If you wonder what is in a person's heart,
just listen to what is expelled from their lips."*

When conducting an investigation during an officer-involved shooting, peace officers are aware they are accountable for every round that leaves their firearm. The position, trajectory, impact—everything! To ensure the use of force was legal, there needs to be justification connected to the decision to squeeze the trigger, regardless of how many times the weapon was fired.

All of the stimuli that filters through the mind comes into play when analyzing whether each round fired was done so legally. What crime was being confronted? What was the suspect doing, or about to do? Were other weapons involved? What was the likely outcome without intervention?

So whether the officer fired once or multiple times, each round needs to be accounted for and legally justified.

Can you imagine if the same standard were applied to the words that are shot from our mouth? We'd all be indicted on criminal charges, and I'd be the first!

Actually, in a spiritual sense, we are! "I tell you, on the day of judgment, people will give account for every careless word they speak," said Jesus, "for by your words you will be justified, and by your words you will be condemned."[1]

If you wonder what is in a person's heart, just listen to what is expelled from their lips. A few verses earlier Jesus said, "[H]ow can you speak good, when you are evil? For out of the abundance of the heart the mouth speaks."[2]

Thank God for his promise, "There is therefore now no condemnation for those who are in Christ Jesus."[3] Otherwise, I'd be guilty beyond a reasonable doubt.

But regardless, we need the wise counsel of King David because the things we say have consequences. "Let the words of my mouth and the meditation of my heart be acceptable in your sight, O Lord, my rock and my redeemer."[4]

---

[1]   Matthew 12:36,37

[2]   Matthew 12:34

[3]   Romans 8:1

[4]   Psalm 19:14

2

CODE FOUR

"King David almost sounds like a frustrated detective unable to capture a group of notorious criminals."

" C ode four—no further assistance necessary! We are 10-15— suspect is in custody!" Those words are music to the ears of peace officers everywhere following a manhunt, pursuit, or other dramatic event leading to the capture of a perpetrator trying to evade authorities.

On October 15 each year, we comment regarding the calendar date, "10/15," while booking a "10-15"—prisoner. So while studying Scripture on October 15 recently, I chuckled while reading Psalm 10:15, which says, "Break the arm of the wicked and evildoer; call his wickedness to account till you find none."

My mind raced to a few violent encounters I had, when injuries occurred during an arrest situation—to cops and the bad guys. But wait, what did King David mean when writing this passage?

As with most verses, it's important to keep them in context. In Psalm 10 David deeply lamented wickedness! He described in great detail the evil devised and calamities caused by evildoers. He asked God for divine intervention. He wanted them "caught in their plots."

King David almost sounds like a frustrated detective unable to capture a group of notorious criminals. By the time you reach v. 15, you can feel his desperation when he pleads with God to cause harm to the wicked.

David clearly thought evil people were acting in contempt of a holy and just God. I am unsure if his request was symbolic or literal, but he certainly hoped God would remove power from the corrupt.

Do you feel the same way? Are you frustrated that malevolence often goes unchecked? Take solace from the words written by David when finishing his thoughts at the end of the chapter. "The Lord is king forever and ever; the nations perish from his land. O Lord, you hear the desire of the afflicted; you will strengthen their heart; you will incline your ear to do justice to the fatherless and the oppressed, so that man who is of the earth may strike terror no more."[5]

God's justice will be complete, but in his timing, not ours. "Vengeance is mine, and recompense, for the time when their foot shall slip; for the day of their calamity is at hand, and their doom comes swiftly."[6]

The reality is that we are all guilty—everyone is "10-15" by nature of our birth in the human race. But Jesus has made things "code four" in a spiritual sense.

Paul the apostle frequently used *shackling* terms when describing those who are not familiar with God. "Formerly, when you did not know God, you were enslaved to those that by nature are not gods."[7]

---

[5] Psalm 10:16–18

[6] Deuteronomy 32:35

[7] Galatians 4:8

But God offered his Son—Jesus, to free us from the guilt derived by enslaving bondage. "We know that our old self was crucified with him in order that the body of sin might be brought to nothing, so that we would no longer be enslaved to sin."[8]

While peace officers say, "Code four," Jesus simply said, "It is finished"[9] as he was sacrificed on our behalf, thus paying a penalty that is owed by each one of us. It was this act of injustice toward Christ that makes perfect justice available to all humankind.

---

[8]   Romans 6:6

[9]   John 19:30

3

SPIRIT OF THE LAW

"Due to civil challenges by those opposing the Christian worldview, many testimonies are sure to find their way to court."

I f you work in law enforcement, you've no doubt heard about enforcing "the spirit of the law" versus "the letter of the law." For instance, the motorist driving 65 mph in a congested 45 mph zone simply because he's late for work is likely to receive a ticket. He violated both the spirit and the letter of the law. But the man driving 65 mph in the same zone while transporting his pregnant wife to the hospital after her water has broken has violated the letter of the law but not the spirit.

The justice system didn't create these terms. They came from the Bible. "But a Jew is one inwardly, and circumcision is a matter of the heart, by the Spirit, not by the letter. His praise is not from man but from God."[10]

The context of this passage is discussing faith, and what it takes to be saved from eternal separation from God. The instruction steers clear of ritualistic acts, but rather the condition of the heart. Do we

---

[10]   Romans 2:29

have a frame of mind willing to follow truth and its' holy ways? Are we obedient inwardly, or simply putting on a show outwardly?

Notice in the passage that "Spirit" is capitalized. In faith, the presence of the Holy Spirit trumps the praise of men (or women). So the next time you hear someone refer to "the spirit" (lower case) versus "the letter of the law," think about the just motivation behind the ordinance versus the authority present (letter of the law) to demand blind conformity. In other words, the spirit of a human law isn't necessarily inspired by the Holy Spirit, so it may or may not be a fair law. But God's laws are always just, because he is the author and creator of life!

Finally, be aware that our religious liberties are being legally assaulted. There are people seeking unjust laws absent "the Spirit," and full of "the letter." Many of the challenges are twisting existing law to fit their agenda. If you visit the websites for Liberty Institute, Alliance Defending Freedom, or the American Center for Law and Justice you would receive a sobering, yet informative education regarding these legal showdowns.[11] The work in process by each organization is to be applauded. I pray it awakens a spiritual renewal for all seeking religious freedom.

Due to civil challenges by those opposing the Christian worldview, many testimonies are sure to find their way to court. Just as the apostle Paul was frequently hauled before Roman courts, providing an opportunity for him to express the gospel of Christ, modern-day believers will as well.

---

[11] www.libertyinstitute.org, www.alliancedefendingfreedom.org, www.aclj.org

4

THE BIG PICTURE

"If Jesus wasn't God, he would have been powerless; no more of a Savior than any other religious figure in history."

What is the big picture in life? Is it religion or politics, two topics most avoid discussing in mixed company? Many people think Jesus came to offer religion and solve politics, but that is untrue. Christ did not come to organize religious rituals—human attempts to reach God—nor did he arrive to solve political battles, international wars, human pandemics, or manmade disasters.

He came to solve two issues that cause the above crisis and the end result from it all—sin and death. To accomplish these tasks he knew there would be turmoil because he was God in the form of man, and this would not be received well, then or now! But if he wasn't God, he would have been powerless; no more of a Savior than any other religious figure in history. Jesus queried, "Do you think I have come to bring peace to the earth?" He knew the answer when he exclaimed, "No, I have come to divide people against each other!

From now on families will be split apart, three in favor of me, and two against—or two in favor and three against."[12]

Jesus does not desire to be a wedge between loved ones, but he knows the condition of the human heart, and it's not pretty. "The heart is deceitful above all things, and desperately sick; who can understand it?"[13] He knew his deity as Christ the Savior divided the Father's cherished creation—all humanity!

Paradoxically, people generally do not want to discuss these topics—Jesus, sin, and death—because of the association to politics and religion. Primarily because we deny the presence of sin, call it by another name, or enjoy the season of destructive hedonism that we find ourselves in. Although we may not believe we have a sin problem, we all have a dilemma with death as it eventually finds each one of us.

I'm not trying to scare anyone into heaven, as I personally do not believe in those tactics. But I am making a concentrated effort to influence everyone to ponder eternity.

While human intelligence can confuse the issue, the Bible is clear. Every indulgent offense and transgression is condemned, and there is a penalty to be paid. Each person who lives and breaths is guilty, regardless of the hallowed halo or rebellious pitchfork represented in our reputations.

Jesus is the perfect sacrifice required to overcome all that is wrong—sin. This is called substitutionary atonement. As we accept the free gift offered by his life, we can claim that which he promised. "Truly, truly, I say to you, whoever hears my word and believes him

---

[12]   Luke 12:51,52

[13]   Jeremiah 17:9

who sent me has eternal life. He does not come into judgment, but has passed from death to life."[14]

That is *The Big Picture!*

---

[14] John 5:24

ROAD TRIP

5

"Your outer shell, despite maintenance issues, will not last forever."

When traveling through desert communities, you will frequently see areas on the shoulder of the highway scorched by intense heat. These markings are evidence that a car was fully engulfed in flames and suffered its demise. Automobiles that likely had preexisting conditions suddenly combust from problems exacerbated by extreme heat. I have become aware of these marks and frequently count them while passing time during long road trips between my home state of California and my current residence in Texas. On a recent drive, I noted as many as six within a ten-mile stretch.

Can this happen to our spiritual life as well? We have a preexisting condition known as the flesh—a nature drawn toward sin. When the heat of a crisis is added to the equation, emotional and spiritual combustion is possible.

We have all seen evidence of this kind—scorched earth—brought about by our natural tendencies.

Whether an automobile is destroyed by fire, or erodes over time, they all wind up scrapped with no hope for life eternal. This is not the case with humanity. "So we do not lose heart. Though our outer self is wasting away, our inner self is being renewed day by day."[15] The renewal begins when a person yields to God's sovereignty and accepts Jesus as Lord and Savior of their life.

Paul's encouragement to the church at Corinth was a dose of reality. Your outer shell, despite maintenance issues, will not last forever. But your soul—inner self—will. He continues in the same letter, "Therefore, if anyone is in Christ, he is a new creation. The old has passed away; behold, the new has come."[16]

Regardless of the number of miles in your life, God has provided an owner's manual—the Bible—to help with your drive and be certain of your eternal destination. Do you refer to God's Word or do you try to Google your way out of trouble?

---

[15]   2 Corinthians 4:16

[16]   2 Corinthians 5:17

THE ELECTRIC CHAIR

6

*"I'd like to move us from a novel
acknowledgement of the cross to a saturating
sense of sacrifice that was made on our behalf."*

A movie, *The Passion of the Christ,* graphically depicted the reality of crucifixion on the cross. My heart leaped at the barbarism depicted in many scenes. But even so, modern culture has sterilized the symbol of the ragged timber called the cross, for all practical purposes.

Jewelry, artwork, and anthems demonstrate the value that people embrace by recognizing the reality of Christ's death. Except time and distance removed from such an event can leave us void of realism.

I'd like to move us from a novel acknowledgement of the cross to a saturating sense of sacrifice that was made on our behalf.

Frequently, it is important to understand the geographical and societal culture in order to comprehend the lessons of Scripture. But now, let's use something from our way of life to appreciate what happened to Jesus. The cross was used to execute condemned men two thousand years ago. Today, the electric chair is still used in some states.

Using this method, the condemned person is strapped in at the wrists, waist, and ankles. An electrode is attached to the head and another to the leg. At least two jolts of an electrical current are applied for several minutes. An initial voltage of about 2,000 volts stops the heart and induces unconsciousness. The body reacts violently and grotesque things occur as death arrives quickly.[17]

It is cruel by the standards of many, yet it is pretty civilized compared to crucifixion on the cross.

Another movie, *The Green Mile*, used the electric chair as a means to execute an inmate for heinous crimes. But the fictional man condemned, John Coffey, was innocent, yet he went willingly to his death. Does this sound familiar? If you saw either movie, your heart ached when witnessing the unjust executions.

So why tell the morbid tale? Because it's important to appreciate the sacrifice that was made on our behalf in order to fully embrace and activate faith that saves us from our own deserved doom.

I have eight songs in iTunes that have the word "cross" in the title.

➢ The Old Rugged Cross
➢ Carry My Cross
➢ Down at the Cross
➢ Lead Me to the Cross
➢ The Power of the Cross
➢ When I Survey the Cross
➢ Shadow of the Cross
➢ The Wonderful Cross

---

[17] http://www.deathpenaltyinfo.org/descriptions-execution-methods – accessed on January 13, 2016.

I enjoy each song, and the words are synchronized with my love and devotion to the Lord. But culturally, we have romanticized the symbol of the cross. Imagine singing *The Old Rugged Electric Chair* or *Lead Me to Ole' Sparky.*

Our sin deserves the electric chair, but thankfully, in faith, I'll embrace the cross. Not the sterile version hanging in our churches, "but with the precious blood of Christ, like that of a lamb without blemish or spot."[18]

Those that oppose godly values claim the Christian faith is driven by guilt. No, my friends, it is faith grounded in gratitude!

"I have been crucified with Christ. It is no longer I who live, but Christ who lives in me. And the life I now live in the flesh I live by faith in the Son of God, who loved me and gave himself for me."[19]

Next time you sing about the cross or place the jewelry around your neck, remember that Christ suffered a more gruesome death than being electrocuted! And he did so willingly, for all of us. Even for those who think faith is driven by shame!

---

[18]   1 Peter 1:19

[19]   Galatians 2:20

SECTION TWO
EVIDENCE TO CONSIDER

7

BEHAVIOR ANALYSIS

"To say James was convinced is an understatement."

*B*ehavior Analysis was one of the more fascinating courses I took during my career in law enforcement. The weeklong educational session brought to life the gut instinct most cops develop about truthfulness and deception, learned when routinely questioning career criminals. But after experiencing the seminar, I was able to articulate why I believed someone was honest or fabricating a story. Analyzing involuntary behavior can affirm the authenticity in a testament, or it tells a story the lips are trying to conceal.

Analyzing behavior of the apostles of Christ has helped to further anchor my faith. Before explaining why, I need to stipulate my belief that the Gospels written by Matthew, Mark, Luke, and John were verified, timely, and accurate. If you are interested in apologetics that examine the facts through an evidentiary lens, I would recommend reading *Cold Case Christianity* by J. Warner Wallace, former homicide detective at the Torrance Police Department in Los Angeles County, and current speaker on the topic.[20] It is a book that followers of Christ will quickly

---

[20] J. Warner Wallace, *Cold Case Christianity* (David C. Cook, 2013).

absorb, and those who are not interested in faith will need to pause and consider the options, because the evidence is overwhelming.

Let's quickly look at James, the brother of Jesus, and analyze his behavior. James—not to be confused with two disciples by the same name—and other family members did not believe Jesus was the Messiah. "For not even his brothers believed in him."[21] Actually it was worse than disbelief. They thought his behavior was irrational. Peter communicated through John Mark who wrote, "[T]hey (his family) went out to seize him, for they were saying, 'He is out of his mind,'"[22] when a crowd gathered around Jesus near their home.

When you believe with absolute certainty something to be incorrect, what does it take to change your mind? For me, it is proof beyond a reasonable doubt, the same standard applied in criminal court.

I believe this was true for James, and Paul knew that when he wrote about the resurrected Christ in a letter to the Corinthians, "Then he (Jesus) appeared to James, then to all the apostles."[23] Jesus had purpose in all he did. Just like he told a doubtful Thomas, "Put your finger here, and see my hands; and put out your hand, and place it in my side. Do not disbelieve, but believe."[24] He also chose to appear to his skeptical brother, James, before appearing to the rest of the apostles.

To say James was convinced is an understatement. First, he doubted his brother. Next he thought Jesus had lost his mental faculties. Did this lead to his absence during the crucifixion when

---

[21] John 7:5

[22] Mark 3:21

[23] 1 Corinthians 15:7

[24] John 20:27

John was left to console Mary? Perhaps! But once James witnessed the resurrected Jesus, you might say he had a paradigm shift. He knew with absolute certainty that Jesus was the Messiah when he began his testament, "James, a servant of God and of the Lord Jesus Christ...."[25]

Those are not the words of a skeptic or doubter, let alone someone who continued to think Jesus needed to be admitted for psychiatric evaluation. Ironically, one of the first messages written by him concern those who doubt. "If any of you lacks wisdom, let him ask God, who gives generously to all without reproach, and it will be given him. But let him ask in faith, with no doubting, for the one who doubts is like a wave of the sea that is driven and tossed by the wind."[26]

What was James' reward for casting doubt aside? Jewish historian Josephus reported that Jewish leaders stoned him to death.[27] Is that behavior consistent with someone perpetuating fraud, deceit, or some massive conspiratorial lie? Not in my book!

James knew his death by stoning would simply begin eternal life. This is behavior that should be analyzed. If your life is like a wave of the sea that is driven and tossed by the wind, perhaps you need to cast aside doubt and come to the same conclusion as James?

---

[25] James 1:1

[26] James 1:5–6

[27] Josephus translated by William Whiston, *Antiquities of the Jews, Book XX* (Kregel Publications, 1971), 423.

8

KILLDEER BIRD

"I believe a killdeer bird willing to play 'chicken' with a John Deere mower, to protect her chicks, is evidence of creative design."

I was on my riding mower in the pasture when I came face-to-face with a killdeer bird. She was bold and howling, with a puffed chest and wings flapping as I approached. She didn't move until the last possible second. Initially I thought she was injured. Once I passed, I realized she was simply "mama" protecting her eggs—and fortunately I did not harm them.

In *The Case for a Creator*,[28] former atheist and legal editor for the Chicago Tribune, Lee Strobel, takes an honest look at the science surrounding evolution and how the facts promulgating Darwin's theory eventually unraveled for him. Once the evidence mounted, Strobel's conclusion came to rest in creative design by a Master Creator—God.

As I pondered the intuitive courage mustered by the killdeer bird protecting her eggs, I wondered what explanation Darwin would offer in regards to maternal instinct?

---

[28]   Lee Strobel, *The Case for a Creator* (Zondervan, 2004).

Darwin's work, *On the Origin of Species,* is preserved online. Chapter 7 is titled *Instinct.* He wrote nearly 12,000 words on the subject. Here are some highlights:

> Instincts comparable with habits, but differ in their origin....... I will not attempt any definition of instinct....... But I could show that none of these characters of instinct are universal....... But I believe that the effects of habit are of quite subordinate importance to the effects of the natural selection of what may be called accidental variations of instincts; that is of variations produced by the same unknown causes which produce slight deviations of bodily structure....... Finally, it may not be a logical deduction, but to my imagination it is far more satisfactory to look at such instincts as the young cuckoo ejecting its foster-brothers, ants making slaves..., the larvae of ichneumonidae feeding within the live bodies of caterpillars, not as specially endowed or created instincts, but as small consequences of one general law, leading to the advancement of all organic beings, namely, multiply, vary, let the strongest live and the weakest die.[29]

His explanation didn't resolve the issue for me. As with much of the theory surrounding evolution, the origin cannot be answered without acknowledging that something (or someone) created it.

As I searched further, I simply found that many of Darwin's successors believe that instinct is nothing more than "unconsciously forming habits." They never answer the question, "What caused the initial behavior that led to a habit?"

Returning to my circumstances in the pasture, I concluded a killdeer bird willing to play "chicken" with a John Deere mower to protect her chicks is evidence of creative design. If not, then

---

[29] http://literature.org/authors/darwin-charles/the-origin-of-species/chapter-07.html – accessed on January 20, 2016

evolution has far more explaining to do than simple mutations that are mathematically impractical.

A mother bird protecting her eggs wasn't the only amazing act of nature that I witnessed. When my female German shepherd gave birth for the first time, she didn't ask for instructions. She separated the umbilical cords, cleaned her pups, and nursed them all without the mentoring of another dog. She did it on her own, with maternal instinct placed in her by a sovereign God.

"For his invisible attributes, namely his eternal power and divine nature, have been clearly perceived, ever since the creation of the world, in the things that have been made. So they are without excuse."[30]

Is it any wonder that social media is wallpapered with pictures of nature? Sunrises, sunsets, mountaintops, snowdrifts, sand dunes, the ocean, fruited plains, killdeer birds, and German shepherds all make the cut by believers and unbelievers alike. These breathtaking pictorials are an example of "divine nature…… clearly perceived."

Can you imagine visiting the Louvre in Paris and admiring a Rembrandt, simply to have the curator tell you there was no artist who created it? I am not sure there is a single person who'd cast faith in such a ridiculous declaration, yet many people do not believe that God exists.

"The heavens declare the glory of God," said King David, "and the sky above proclaims his handiwork."[31]

---

[30] Romans 1:20

[31] Psalm 19:1

His son, King Solomon taught, "[H]e (God) has put eternity into man's heart, ..."[32] Is it any wonder that those who cast God aside still try to answer questions regarding life after death?

I'm not looking to debate people who disagree, I simply prefer to take it in and worship the Creator! This is God's *Justice Revealed!*

---

[32] Ecclesiastes 3:11

ONE EARTH

9

"Throughout history the Bible has remained constant and infallible, while textbooks need to be updated annually as data changes."

In 1829 Sir Robert Peel established the first Metropolitan Police Force in London based at Scotland Yard. The constables employed were affectionately known as "Bobbies."

Based upon the singular and plural nouns used in the opening statement, you know there was one police force but more than one constable, right?

Track with me on this!

"In the beginning, God created the heavens, and the earth."[33] Scientists have pondered whether there are other planets that contain life, or more specifically, is there another earth? If so, this would have significant ramifications in God's plan and Jesus' sacrifice as outlined in Scripture. If another inhabited planet were discovered, would this degrade the creation account in the Bible?

Aside from the scientific improbability that human life could exist anywhere but our current placement in the solar system, I have

---

[33] Genesis 1:1

frequently positioned my belief in the simplicity of Genesis 1:1. The word "heavens" is plural but "earth" is singular. If human life existed anywhere else but planet earth, would God have told us so?

In a passage unrelated to Genesis 1, the apostle Paul highlights the importance of the singular as opposed to the plural when he wrote, "Now the promises were made to Abraham and to his offspring. It does not say, 'And to offsprings,' referring to many, but referring to one, 'And to your offspring,' who is Christ."[34]

Paul referenced Genesis 12:7 when the singular term "offspring" was used, and he emphasizes this fact when he wrote, "[I]t does not say, 'And to offsprings....'"

Biblical authors mention "heavens" (plural) and "earth" (singular) in the same passage eighty-four times, and "heaven" (singular) and "earth" (singular) are combined another 104 times. While "heaven" is used in the singular and plural forms, "earth" is always singular.[35]

While science continues to prove the Bible accurate, I believe efforts trying to locate another humanly inhabited earth are in vain based upon the singular use of "earth" in Genesis—and throughout the Bible—as well as Paul's emphasis on the importance of the singular as opposed to plural nouns in his letter to the Galatians.

I understand that I'm proposing a theological argument to a scientific question. But throughout history the Bible has remained constant and infallible, while textbooks require annual updates as data changes. I know this will be insufficient evidence for skeptics, but the Bible has never contradicted new discoveries. Prominent theologian

---

[34] Galatians 3:16

[35] https://www.biblegateway.com/quicksearch/?quicksearch= heaven+and+earth&qs_version=ESV – accessed on January 2, 2016.

and author Wayne Grudem said, "New scientific or historical facts may cause us to reexamine our interpretation of Scripture, but they will never directly contradict Scripture."[36]

---

[36]   Wayne A. Grudem, *Christian Beliefs*, (Zondervan, 2005), 15.

WITNESS CREDIBILITY

*"'Because it was unique and significant,'
was my reply."*

"Auntie, I'm going to the big house," were comments I overheard a murder suspect say during a homicide investigation. "Gonna be with Uncle Johnny. Gonna be gone a long time." Shortly after hearing the unsolicited comment, I included it with my investigative report.

When I was called to the witness stand a few years later, I provided testimony to the words that I heard. "How can you remember his statement so precisely?" asked the prosecutor.

"Because it was unique and significant," was my reply.

The defense attorney challenged my answer. "How can you be certain that you remembered his words accurately?" he inquired.

"Because I memorialized his utterance in my report," I answered, attempting to sound impressive before the crowded courtroom. *I wrote it down, word for word*, is what I should have said.

Do you realize that is how the Gospels came to be? Matthew, Mark, Luke, and John witnessed events that were unique and significant. Shortly after these events came to be, they were written about—memorialized—in firsthand accounts.

John, one of Jesus' closest disciples, gave witness to dialogue between Jesus, Thomas, and Philip. As you will probably recognize, the content of this conversation changed the course of history.

"Let not your hearts be troubled. Believe in God; believe also in me. In my Father's house are many rooms. If it were not so, would I have told you that I go to prepare a place for you? And if I go and prepare a place for you, I will come again and will take you to myself, that where I am you may be also. And you know the way to where I am going." Thomas said to him, "Lord, we do not know where you are going. How can we know the way?" Jesus replied, "I am the way, and the truth, and the life. No one comes to the Father except through me. If you had known me, you would have known my Father also. From now on you do know him and have seen him."

Philip said to him, "Lord, show us the Father, and it is enough for us." Jesus said to him, "Have I been with you so long, and you still do not know me, Philip? Whoever has seen me has seen the Father. How can you say, 'Show us the Father'? Do you not believe that I am in the Father and the Father is in me? The words that I say to you I do not speak on my own authority, but the Father who dwells in me does his works. Believe me that I am in the Father and the Father is in me, or else believe on account of the works themselves.

"Truly, truly, I say to you, whoever believes in me will also do the works that I do; and greater works than these will he do, because I am going to the Father. Whatever you ask in my name, this I will do, that the Father may be glorified in the Son. If you ask me anything in my name, I will do it."[37]

---

[37] John 14:1–14

John was an eyewitness to these events; contemporaries and successors alike have corroborated his words. No one has ever shown him to be inaccurate, and he knew his boldness would come at a great personal sacrifice—perhaps the most compelling attribute of all. He would be a *dream witness* by contemporary standards.

Let me put this in perspective. If a citizen came forward with information regarding a gang-related homicide, and although he was previously terrified, agreed to testify, a prosecutor would be thrilled. With nothing to gain and ultimately his life to lose, there isn't a juror who would discount his testimony. That best describes the plight of the apostles. Empowered by the Holy Spirit, they told what they knew to be true.

If John were questioned on the witness stand today, he could provide the same answers that I gave. The circumstances were *unique and significant*, and he wrote about them a short time later! I believe John was a credible witness. Do you?

SECTION THREE
ELEMENTS OF FAITH

11

K9 ALERT

"God made dogs to sense with their nose, and Christians to detect by faith."

I had the opportunity to work undercover operations for ten years. I enjoyed the challenges from this assignment as it meant proactive enforcement in the area of narcotics, gangs, vice, and major crimes.

We often used narcotic detecting canines (K9) when searching for drugs. It was always a thrill to see one of our dogs alert to a hiding spot that would never have been found otherwise.

I have a funny memory of a K9 alerting to the crotch of a drug trafficker during a search warrant service. The handler had to restrain the positive reaction by the police service dog (PSD) while the dealer happily volunteered the stash secreted in his Under Armour. The crook literally thought his manhood was going to be mauled.

Unlike their human companions, K9's search with their nose. Sight is often third in the line of senses used by a dog, behind smell and hearing.

Christians err when they use vision as the primary sensory preceptor when following Christ, since it is written, "For we walk by faith, not by sight."[38]

God made dogs to sense with their nose, and Christians to detect by faith. Neither is done blindly as Matthew, the tax collector turned disciple, wrote, "But blessed are your eyes, for they see, and your ears, for they hear."[39]

Faith in God's Word should be used primarily as we navigate the course set before us, and then corroborated using other senses. When *faith* in truth is at the helm, we are less likely to wander off course and become confused or lost.

---

[38]   2 Corinthians 5:7

[39]   Matthew 13:16

12

THE WEDDING FEAST

"If someone didn't respond to our invitation to attend my daughter's wedding, they didn't dine with us."

One of the greatest time-honored traditions in the military is cutting the cake celebrating the Marine Corps' birthday. The traditional passing of cake from the oldest to the youngest Marine demonstrates the passing of the honor, experience, and heart of the corps to the next generation of Marines to carry on. If you've participated in or witnessed the ritual, you are aware of the solemn formality of the event.

Recently I was asked the question, "What is the purpose of life?"

I believe it's to prepare for eternity. Not with ritualism building a pyramid to God, but a relationship that I'm drawn into with Christ Jesus! Everything done through this relational scope, whether for yourself or others, is preparing for eternity.

The next logical question would be, "How do you do that?"

We have all attended a wedding. As father of the bride, I came to appreciate the planning and preparation that goes into the event. When it was time for the meal, those who declined the invitation did not dine with us. (Factually, that's a bit misleading as we had several *wedding crashers,* but you get the point!)

As it relates to your purpose in life, consider what Christ taught:

> And again Jesus spoke to them in parables, saying, "The kingdom of heaven may be compared to a king who gave a wedding feast for his son, and sent his servants to call those who were invited to the wedding feast, but they would not come."[40]

The Marines *cut the cake* as a way to honor those who've responded to the call of duty! But not all have responded, so not everyone gets to participate.

If someone didn't respond to our invitation to attend my daughter's wedding, they missed out. Jesus said heaven can be compared to a wedding feast, but only those who respond to the invitation will be allowed to remain. There will be no wedding crashers in heaven. The parable continues:

> But when the king came in to look at the guests, he saw there a man who had no wedding garment. And he said to him, "Friend, how did you get in here without a wedding garment?" And he was speechless. Then the king said to the attendants, "Bind him hand and foot and cast him into the outer darkness. In that place there will be weeping and gnashing of teeth."[41]

So what is the purpose of life? It is to prepare for the wedding feast! After personally responding to God's invitation, we should make it a priority to check with others hoping they will attend as well.

While living temporally in this life, I desire to perpetually prepare for the heavenly banquet by connecting to the source of life. He

---

[40]   Matthew 22:1-3

[41]   Matthew 22:11–13

has passed along a timeless series of letters canonized into one book—the Bible. Without question, it is the most elaborate wedding invitation of all time! Scripture is instructive and intuitive because it was authored under the divine inspiration of our Creator—the Father of the bride.

Attention military veterans and friends serving in law enforcement, you've been invited—along with all others. Will you respond? If your call to duty has frozen your heart, allow the love of God to thaw it out. "For God so loved the world, that he gave his only Son, that whoever believes in him should not perish but have eternal life."[42]

---

[42] John 3:16

FOR ME TO LIVE IS CHRIST

13

*"While continuing my workout,
the Lord worked me over."*

I have been riding motorcycles for the better part of forty years. "LIVE TO RIDE" is scripted on one of my workout shirts. While training in the gym recently, I felt a keen sense of awareness of the message.

My attention was drawn to a solid young man training hard nearby. As I viewed his prosthetic leg, I was uncomfortable by the words that were a clear *overstatement* of the ethos I represent. "Like To Ride" would be more appropriate. I thought there was a day in the not too distant past that the young man probably pondered, *Live to walk again…… someday…… maybe?*

As my mind considered the words on my shirt, "Live To Ride," and the thoughts I attributed to the gentleman, "live to walk again," I reflected on something written to the Philippians, "For me to live is Christ…."

While continuing my workout, the Lord worked me over. I believe the Holy Spirit wanted me to affirm a man who apparently lost a leg in war, an assumption I made based upon my observations.

But interrupting someone's momentum violates workout etiquette, not to mention my focus was on his prosthesis, something I'm sure he tried to avoid.

Eventually, I approached and directed my attention to his leg. "Combat injury?" I asked.

"Yes. I was a Marine serving in the Middle East," he politely replied as we began a brief conversation.

We exchanged names and I told him I'd like to hear more of his story if he desired to share it. I concluded our chat by thanking him for his service and sacrifice. I don't know what this meant to him, but I knew I was obediently following through on instructions from the Lord—gym impropriety or not!

"For me to live is Christ, and to die is gain,"[43] Paul wrote to the church at Philippi as he reflected on the abundant life possessed following his dramatic conversion.

As a follower of Christ, I have been sanctified. That means I've been set apart for holiness. It is through the process of spiritual maturity that I am developed and used as God calls.

Think of a long block of wood that has not yet been sculpted. Before it is crafted, it is not very useful, and it certainly is not designed to be a baseball bat. But once the skilled woodworker spins it on the lathe, grinds away the unwanted excess material, and then beautifully shapes the piece of lumber into a *Louisville Slugger*, it is sanctified in a sense. It has been set apart and designed to serve a specific purpose—hit baseballs.

John MacArthur is the pastor-teacher of Grace Community Church in Sun Valley, California, as well as an author, conference speaker, president of the Master's College and Seminary, and

---

[43]   Philippians 1:21

featured teacher with the Grace to You media ministry. His teaching is instructive as he outlines the basic steps of biblical sanctification.

> The first is *cognition*. God's pattern for spiritual growth starts with understanding what the Bible says and what it means....... True sanctification begins with renewing your mind.......
>
> Cognition leads to a second step: *conviction*. As you grow in your understanding of the Bible, you begin to develop convictions out of that understanding.......
>
> The third step in the biblical process of sanctification is *affection*. Throughout Scripture we see over and over that God's people truly love His truth.......
>
> But you won't truly love God's Word if it's not already shaping the way you live. And it can't shape the way you live if you don't know it. That's why any methods or patterns for spiritual growth that don't start with the study of God's truth cannot lead you to true sanctification.[44]

Returning to my previous illustration; if God is the Woodworker and I'm the lumber, he shapes me into a *Louisville Slugger* using cognition—helping me understand the Bible, conviction—developing a sense of right and wrong based upon my understanding of Scripture, and affection—drawing me closer so I love his truth.

The author of Hebrews wrote, "For by a single offering he has perfected for all time those who are being sanctified."[45] As such, I don't "live to ride," but I "live for Christ." What do you live for?

---

[44] http://www.gty.org/blog/B120913/the-steps-of-biblical-sanctification – accessed on January 21, 2016

[45] Hebrews 10:14

14

YOU'RE FIRED......
OR NOT!

"God revealed the truth of the nature of Christ to us; he's calling us to respond in faith, and then we commit ourselves to the Lord......or not."

"You're fired!" Two words you never want to hear. Let me tell a story of someone who was *unfired* in order to illustrate the biblical concept of redemptive salvation.

Working as the patrol division watch commander, I was called into the chief's office to discuss a probationary officer who wasn't cutting it. "This was the final day for Johnson (not his actual name) to turn it around," commented the chief of police. "Will he make it, or is it time to cut him loose?"

"Sadly, I'm afraid it's time, boss," I replied. "We've spent months working with him. Every attempt at proficiency has failed. Some people simply are not cut out for this line of work. He's struggling in nearly every area."

"All right, I'll call him in and let him know that we're going to let him go. In the meantime, will you ensure his police unit is cleaned out? I don't want to give him access once he's been terminated."

"You got it. I'll send him over."

Thirty minutes later, Johnson came out of the chief's office. He returned to his unit only to find it cleaned out. About that time the chief summoned me once again. "I decided to keep Johnson," he said. "I want to give him another chance."

"Really?" I said surprisingly. "Did he know that you planned to terminate him?"

"Sure. I told him he deserved to be fired. I even asked if he wanted to resign in lieu of termination. But after talking for a bit, I decided to give him another chance. Needless to say he leaped at the opportunity."

"Well, I'm sure he did. It's not every day you get unfired."

"Indeed it is not. Let's see if he makes the most of the opportunity."

From this illustration, I hope you were able to grasp that Johnson deserved to be fired. But the chief called him to his office and offered him a second chance. Johnson said yes! It was unmerited favor.

Professionally, Johnson received a reprieve from the chief, just as we can spiritually receive redemptive salvation from God. We do not deserve to spend eternity with him in heaven due to sin in our life, but he revealed the truth of the nature of Christ to us; he's calling us to respond in faith, and then we commit ourselves to the Lord...... or not. It isn't a negotiation, it's simply an offer.

Writing to the church at Ephesus, Paul explains it well,

> But God, being rich in mercy, because of the great love with which he loved us, even when we were dead in our trespasses, made us alive together with Christ—by grace you have been saved—and raised us up with him and seated us with him in the heavenly places in Christ Jesus, so that in the coming ages he might show the immeasurable riches of his grace in kindness toward us in Christ Jesus. For by grace you have been saved

through faith. And this is not your own doing; it is the gift of God, not a result of works, so that no one may boast.[46]

By God's grace, I've been *unfired* too!

---

[46] Ephesians 2:4–9

15

BY FAITH

"We had to exercise faith that our strategy was solid and we could execute the plan with a measured amount of safety."

When preparing a high-risk raid, we completed an *Operational Plan* (OP) at my police department. The OP contained logistics, assignments, and contingencies. It didn't matter if the intended target was a murder suspect, violent gang member, or armed drug dealer. We uniquely tailored the OP preparing for each encounter.

When planning such a raid, we sought to uncover every known fact in order to gain a tactical advantage. For the most extreme incursions, we rehearsed our movements hoping to fine-tune the effort.

No matter how much logical planning we put into an operation, ultimately we had to exercise faith that our strategy was solid and we could execute the plan with a measured amount of safety, fully understanding that calculated risks were (are) part of the business.

I thought of this process while reading Hebrews 11. *Faith in action* is the theme of this chapter.

"Now faith is the assurance of things hoped for, the conviction of things not seen."[47]

Dictionary definitions of "faith" include "belief or trust." I found it interesting that the author of Hebrews described faith as "assurance and conviction." The dictionary definition leaves room for doubt. But Hebrews looked at faith with absolute certainty.

I appreciate and value apologetics—defense of the Christian faith. Using sports as my analogy, I actually view apologetics as being on *offense*. I marvel at the painstaking investigative research of so many. It provides a logical foundation by which we can stand upon. But ultimately, faith is still required because there is a supernatural element that defies logic. I'm all right with that, and I assert it into my conversations since I firmly believe it takes greater faith to follow belief systems that offer more questions than answers.

If I could explain God's omniscient, omnipresent, and omnipotent capability, I would be God. If he didn't possess those traits, he would be limited and we'd all be in trouble.

If you have faith, did proof lead to your conclusion, or did you possess it regardless? God can reveal himself anyway he chooses! When asked, "Why are you a Christian?" my response is simple: "Because it's true."

Is your faith the dictionary definition—belief and trust—or the Biblical application—assurance and conviction?

Walk through Hebrews 11 with me and check out the faith of Old Testament saints described by the author:

➢ By faith Abel offered a more acceptable sacrifice than Cain (v. 4).

---

[47]   Hebrews 1:1

➢ By faith Enoch was taken up so he would not see death (v. 5).

➢ By faith Noah constructed the ark (v. 7).

➢ By faith Abraham obeyed when he was called out to receive an inheritance (v. 8).

➢ By faith Abraham went to live in the land of promise (v. 9).

➢ By faith Sarah received power to conceive (v. 11).

➢ By faith Abraham offered Isaac (v. 17).

➢ By faith Isaac invoked future blessings on Jacob and Esau (v. 20).

➢ By faith Jacob blessed each of the sons of Joseph (v. 21).

➢ By faith, Joseph mentioned the exodus of the Israelites (v. 22).

➢ By faith Moses, when he was born, was hidden for three months by his parents (v. 23).

➢ By faith Moses, when he was grown, refused to be called the son of pharaoh's daughter (v. 24).

➢ By faith, Moses left Egypt unafraid of the anger of the king (v. 27).

➢ By faith, Moses kept the Passover and sprinkled the blood so the Destroyer of the firstborn might not touch them (v. 28).

➢ By faith, the people crossed the Red Sea as on dry land (v. 29).

➢ By faith, the walls of Jericho fell down (v. 30).

➢ By faith, Rahab the prostitute did not perish because of her obedience (v. 31).

➢ By faith, Gideon, Barak, Samson, Jephthah, David, Samuel, and the prophets conquered kingdoms, enforced justice, obtained promises, stopped the mouths of lions, quenched the power of fire, escaped the edge of the sword, were made strong out of weakness, became mighty in war, and put foreign armies to flight (vv. 32–34).

With the exception of Enoch, each Old Testament saint died in faith. "[G]od is not ashamed to be called their God, for he has prepared for them a city."[48]

But the author tells the Hebrews that God had provided some better things for them. The gospel of Jesus Christ is the end and perfection of the Old Testament. Without the gospel, the church would have remained in an incomplete and imperfect state.

I consider the dictionary definition of "faith"—belief and trust—to be curing like wet cement. It is movable. But Biblical faith—assurance and conviction—is anchored in dried concrete! It is immovable!

God has a *faith plan* for you and me. This is what he tells us:

> ➤ By faith, you can understand creation.[49]
> ➤ By faith, you can be saved.[50]
> ➤ By faith, you can overcome the obstacles of the world.[51]
> ➤ By faith, you can do exactly what God places before you.[52]

By faith I pray your belief and trust become *assurance* and *conviction*. From assurance comes *hope,* and with conviction is *action.* We need Christian men and women to spread hope and answer the call to action—*By Faith*!

---

[48]   Hebrews 11:16

[49]   Hebrews 11:3

[50]   Ephesians 2:8–9

[51]   1 John 5:4

[52]   Matthew 17:20

SECTION FOUR
COUNSELING SESSION

STEWARD YOUR INFLUENCE

16

"Biblical knowledge without action is arrogant disobedience."

Have you had a river of tears streaming from your eyes at a memorial service because the person being honored had such a profound impact on your life?

Would you like to steward the influence you have on others, but you're unsure how to do it?

It's the coaching, counseling, mentoring concepts to *pay it forward* with no expectation of reward that make a difference. How can you duplicate these actions for those around you?

I find it interesting that James, the brother of Jesus, sat on the sidelines in doubt during Christ's ministry years. It was only after witnessing the resurrected Messiah that James was motivated by faith into action as mentioned previously.

He writes, "But be doers of the word, and not hearers only, deceiving yourselves."[53] He later continues, "So whoever knows the right thing to do and fails to do it, for him it is sin."[54]

---

[53] James 1:22

[54] James 4:17

So we need to "know the right thing to do," and be "doers of the word." To accomplish these objectives, we need to be connected to God and his blueprint for us.

Have you tried to spread cold, hard butter on toast? If you're like me, you probably succeed in mutilating the bread while leaving landmines all over. But when the butter has been warmed to room temperature, it softens and spreads with ease. Such is the case with our hearts! They need to be softened to be effective and understand all that God has for us.

Don't worry! God is in the business of performing heart transplants. "And I will give you a new heart, and a new spirit I will put within you. And I will remove the heart of stone from your flesh and give you a heart of flesh. And I will put my Spirit within you, and cause you to walk in my statutes and be careful to obey my rules."[55]

The call is simple. Biblical knowledge without action is arrogant disobedience. Action with a softened heart for the Lord is serving others in his name—ministry—and that is how you *Steward Your Influence!*

---

[55]   Ezekiel 36:26,27

MASTER OF THE HOUSE

17

"More often than not, time is present if we manage events with a critical eye for productive usefulness."

I am the master of two beautiful black German shepherds. I have raised and trained them from pups. I have showered them with love and affection, and watched out for their best interests. I feed them what they need, not what they can wildly devour. I bathe and groom them for their health and welfare.

Mako and *Maya* have inside privileges at my house. Because of this, they tend to follow me everywhere. Regardless of my location they are nearby, ready to serve and play as I command.

When I see them recline at my feet and then jump to follow as I move, I often think, *What a picture of servitude*, followed by the question, *Do I follow my Master with the same loyalty and devotion?*

"No one can serve two masters," proclaimed Jesus, "for either he will hate the one and love the other, or he will be devoted to the one and despise the other. You cannot serve God and money."[56] Different translations use the word, "mammon" or "wealth" in

---

[56] Matthew 6:24

lieu of "money." In essence, love of possessions can hinder your relationship with God.

Is it possible that most of the American Christian culture is in denial? We denounce the belief that we have an unhealthy devotion to something, yet remove it from our lives and we're lost or crushed.

There is a surefire test that can be used to determine the real master in your life. Examine where you spend your disposable time and income. This can be revealing and painful if you're willing to accept the evidence. I know—I've been there!

Some mockingly reply, "Disposable time? Income? What is that?"

God can help us discern between fruitful activity versus mind-numbing entertainment when our heart is aligned with his. Start with the TV, time surfing the web, and the volume of hours being entertained on social media. Regardless of busyness, if you idolize something, you'll find a way to fit it in. More often than not, time is present if we manage events with a critical eye for productive usefulness.

If you're brave enough to take this test, it will help you analyze and reconnect with the one who desires to be the *Master of the House.* It's a freewill choice that God has given us. Choose wisely!

18

REPROOF

"Until they recognize Jesus as Lord and Savior, their amorality is not immorality in their eyes."

As a young adult, I was fed up with hymns. In my mind I *tolerated* enough of them during my developmental years. With the wisdom of youth, I enjoyed the *enlightenment* of new worship music.

As I've matured in life and in faith, I've come full circle. The lyrics capturing theological truth from some of the classics have become prized counsel to me. *My Jesus, I Love Thee* is one example. As I recently sang the second verse during a church service, I felt a lump in my throat as I pondered my personal history.

For those who've read *The Spirit behind Badge 145*, you know my story. I was *The Prodigal Son* in my mid twenties. My life was filled with narcissism and infidelity. I briefly mention the details here because I want to make a point about a verse that is quoted out of context far too often by people who otherwise have no idea what the Bible really says.

"Judge not that you be not judged."[57] How many times have you heard someone from pop culture refer to it? Usually as ammunition

---

[57] Matthew 7:1

against a Christian. We have been inundated with people afraid to take a stand. The phrase "I'm not judging" has become a tagline everywhere you turn, as if suggesting good choices are somehow inconsiderate.

Let's put the verse in context. It is followed by the admonition, "Why do you see the speck that is in your brother's eye, but do not notice the log that is in your own eye? Or how can you say to your brother, 'Let me take the speck out of your eye,' when there is the log in your own eye? You hypocrite, first take the log out of your own eye, and then you will see clearly to take the speck out of your brother's eye."[58]

Let me apply this in the real world scenario that is my life. Nearly three decades ago I had no spiritual authority to confront a brother or sister in Christ involved in sin because I had a "log" in my own eye. Actually, I had an entire forest! But I submitted to God's will and turned from my destructive nature. His grace took over and I was restored to a right relationship with the Lord and my wife. Fidelity has been my sobriety since 1992. I have since had many conversations of counsel with men engaged in sexual sin—any act of sex outside of marriage between a man and a woman. By the way, that is God's standard, and I concur. Moreover, it's nonnegotiable unless you discard portions of his inerrant Word—something that is happening with greater frequency.

Scripture calls for reproof. It's an *old-fashioned* word that simply means to "disapprove and rebuke." Proverbs says with reproof comes intelligence, wisdom, and prudence. Honor will also find those who receive it. Make no mistake, this means we are to take a scriptural

---

[58]   Matthew 7:3–5

stand on moral issues with those who claim to be followers of Jesus. We are to offer reproof!

For those who still doubt the church has a responsibility to *police* itself, consider the following Scripture:

So if you are offering your gift at the altar and there remember that your brother has something against you, leave your gift there before the altar and go. First be reconciled to your brother, and then come and offer your gift.[59]

If your brother sins against you, go and tell him his fault, between you and him alone. If he listens to you, you have gained your brother. But if he does not listen, take one or two others along with you, that every charge may be established by the evidence of two or three witnesses. If he refuses to listen to them, tell it to the church. And if he refuses to listen even to the church, let him be to you as a Gentile and a tax collector.[60]

But now I am writing to you not to associate with anyone who bears the name of brother if he is guilty of sexual immorality or greed, or is an idolater, reviler, drunkard, or swindler—not even to eat with such a one. For what have I to do with judging outsiders? Is it not those inside the church whom you are to judge? God judges those outside. "Purge the evil person from among you."[61]

As for those who persist in sin, rebuke them in the presence of all, so that the rest may stand in fear.[62]

---

[59]   Matthew 5:23–24
[60]   Matthew 18:15–17
[61]   1 Corinthians 5:11–13
[62]   1 Timothy 5:20

For those who do not believe the message of the cross, my response is entirely different. If I have a relationship with such a person, I simply offer my opinion that their amoral decision(s) will ultimately crumble. If I have no emotional bank account with people outside of Christ, I keep my opinions and reproof to myself because I expect them to live as they are. It doesn't mean I don't want the best for them. But until they recognize Jesus as Lord and Savior, their amorality is not immorality in their eyes.

Taking a stand for moral behavior as it relates to public policy is another discussion, yet I always support plans and vote according to biblical principles.

Back to the church service and singing, the second verse to *My Jesus, I Love Thee.*

> I love Thee because Thou has first loved me,
> And purchased my pardon on Calvary's tree.
> I love Thee for wearing the thorns on Thy brow;
> If ever I loved Thee, my Jesus, 'tis now.

In the words of one of my favorite legal scholars and law enforcement trainers, Associate Justice Bill Bedsworth, from the Fourth District Court of Appeal in California, "For right now, that's all she wrote!"

19

DEFAULT SETTINGS

"It has become fashionable to alter (God's) instruction to meet societal choices that are incongruous with the timeless treasure of truth."

Have you typed a message simply to have the AutoCorrect feature in your device change a word, and in doing so, change the meaning altogether? I once intended to write, "Let's be right" and it turned into "Let's be ridiculous."

One letter or digit can alter your intent. On another occasion, I meant to encourage a group to abide in the instructions given by the apostle James, "Therefore, confess your sins to one another and pray for one another, that you may be healed," as outlined in James 5:16. But rather than quoting the passage, I incorrectly wrote where it could be found—James 5:6. When I verified the words in James 5:6, I discovered, "You have condemned and murdered the righteous person"—a significantly different message!

In life, we all have *auto* features that can bring damage if left unchecked and unfiltered. Mine include aggressively cutting, impulsive responses. Our automatic response features need to be measured by our *default settings*.

There are many factors that contribute to a habitual reaction. But as a follower of Christ, the only one that matters is God's Word. Paul wrote to his protégé, Timothy, "All Scripture is breathed out by God and profitable for teaching, for reproof, for correction, and for training in righteousness, "[63]

Not part, but *all* of it!

While culture changes, God's Word remains the same. It has become fashionable to alter his instruction to meet societal choices that are incongruous with the timeless treasure of truth.

Will your *Default Settings* be found in Scripture or a new way of life being defined by those who disagree with God or others who twist the truth?

---

[63]   2 Timothy 3:16

20

TOMORROW

"Tomorrow is better than 'later' and certainly superior to 'never.'"

" Tomorrow!" exclaimed my then five-year-old grandson, Dax, and everyone burst into laughter. But what was the question? Recently my family sat around the dinner table celebrating my daughter's birthday. As is often the case, we created a game to encourage meaningful interaction. The questions were posed; "If you could change the date you were born to any day of the year, what would it be? Would you like your birthday to be near or far from the major holidays? How about a different season?"

As the answers were given, Dax was taking it in. Although he's young, he has quickly associated birthday celebrations with loving attention and gifts. So while everyone else provided a specific calendar date as his or her answer, Dax said, "Tomorrow!"

If Jesus asked us to select one day in the next year to spend some personal time with him, how would we respond? Would we need to clear our calendar or wait for the perfect occasion? Is there a season that is preferable, or would our answer match that of Dax?

With inspiration from a five-year-old, "tomorrow"—and everyday—is my response. Jesus provides the unconditional love, direction, affirmation, guidance, and counsel that are unparalleled. There is an exhaustive list of gifts that he offers to include those most familiar: love, joy, peace, hope, forgiveness, grace, salvation, etc… but the gifts continue with spiritual protection, security, sound mind, objective truth, and mercy, among others.

"Why put off until tomorrow what can be accomplished today?" goes the axiom. But with urgency, I recommend, "tomorrow is better than 'later' and certainly superior to 'never.'"

21

THE SABBATH

"Find time to mentally rest and draw near to the throne of grace."

D o you feel exhausted? Are you at wit's end fearing there are not enough hours in the day or days in the week? Does the daily news have you down? Would you like to receive mercy and find grace in time of need?

The author of Hebrews explains what we need to do as God's children. He expressly repeated what Moses instructed in Exodus, "Remember the Sabbath day, to keep it holy."

Is the answer that simple? According to Hebrews 4, it is. While I'm not going to rewrite the entire passage, I would like to share my observations from the text:

> ➤ "[T]he promise of entering his rest still stands...." (v. 1)
> The practice of rest on the Sabbath is not merely part of the Old Testament law. It should be part of our practice today.
> ➤ "[L]et us fear lest any of you failed to reach it." (v. 1)
> We should respect the practice.

- ➢ "For we who have believed enter that rest...." (v. 3)
  Obedience means receiving rest.
- ➢ "[T]hey shall not enter my rest...." (v. 3 and repeated in v. 5 as quoted from Psalm 95:11)
  Disobedience means being separated from God's rest.
- ➢ "And God rested on the seventh day...." (v. 4)
  God established the principle of rest.
- ➢ "[F]ailed to enter because of disobedience...." (v. 6)
  Disregarding the practice equals disobedience.
- ➢ "So then, there remains a Sabbath rest for the people of God...." (v. 9)
  The principle of rest is reinforced.
- ➢ "For whoever has entered God's rest has also rested from his works as God did from his." (v. 10)
  Put work on hold.
- ➢ "[S]trive to enter that rest, so that no one may fall by the same sort of disobedience." (v. 11)
  It should be a goal to help avoid sin.
- ➢ "Let us then with confidence draw near to the throne of grace, that we may receive mercy and find grace to help in time of need." (v. 16)
  The benefits of practicing the Sabbath.

We live in a culture that has destroyed practicing the Sabbath! Some things are mandatory, but most are not.

When work requires your presence on Sunday, be mindful it is the practice of the Sabbath that God designed, not a ritual peddling you closer to the Father.

When the Pharisees accused Jesus of breaking the Sabbath, he responded to them, "The Sabbath was made for man, not man for the Sabbath. So the Son of Man is lord even of the Sabbath."[64]

So find time to mentally rest and draw near to the throne of grace even if you are required to work each Sunday. If you do, you are assured to receive mercy and find grace to help in time of need. This is a promise from God that is worth claiming!

---

[64]   Mark 2:27, 28

SECTION FIVE
CORE VALUES

OUR FAMILY WAS PREGNANT

22

*"When a teen in the home is expecting a baby,
the entire family is pregnant!"*

Jim (Dad): When a seventeen-year-old high school girl from a home practicing biblical principles becomes pregnant, it's like an angry mule that kicks, and everyone feels the impact.

My wife, Jamie, and I married in 1983. Brenna was our first child, born in 1989. Two boys, Brock in 1991 and Jordan in 1993, followed her. Brenna was a cute little blonde delight. I often thought one of my strengths as a father was showing affection to my children. I believed this strength would be a key ingredient that would steer my daughter away from teenage pregnancy. I was wrong.

This is Brenna's story, but I believe you'll find value hearing from the entire family, because when a teen in the home is expecting a baby, the entire family is pregnant!

Brenna: No matter what her beliefs or how she was raised, if a pregnant teen tells you she never seriously contemplated all of her *options*, she's probably not telling the truth. I was seventeen, a senior in high school, and had no idea what I was going to do. I was raised in a Christian home, but chose to rebel and allowed myself to be deceived and enticed by sin. I became pregnant, and distress was part of my daily routine.

My boyfriend Ryan and I finally reached the point where we decided we loved each other and were going to try to figure it out. With our stomach in knots, we told our parents.

Jim (Dad): The news slapped the self-righteousness right out of me. How could this happen in my family? I thought I had done everything right as the spiritual leader in my home; not perfect, but generally kept us on the right path.

I sought oxygen, but couldn't find any! "A slow boil," best describes the internal combustion I experienced.

Brenna's options included giving birth, adoption, or abortion. Once I learned of her pregnancy, giving birth was the only option in my mind. But God immediately impressed upon me to adopt this child if they chose that route. Intuitively I knew my daughter would one day want to be part of this baby's life, and I could not imagine my grandchild being raised by someone else when we had the love and resources to do so.

Brenna: There was a lot of praying and crying. Looking back, the amount of support and love we were shown instantly by our parents is both rare, and significantly linked to the success we have as parents and now a married couple. We are not naive to the statistics; we know many others who unfortunately didn't make it. They are left dealing with court dates, child support, angry exes, and all the other baggage that comes with raising a child without the foundation of a Christ-centered home and marriage.

Jim (Dad): I was taken to task over hounding Brenna with the statistics saying their relationship would not survive. Several weeks into the pregnancy, and in tears, Brenna told me she knew but didn't need to be reminded every day. "We will be the exception," she expressed as her face said, *Please love me regardless.*

"There is no such thing as an accidental baby," my own mother reminded me.

> For you formed my inward parts;
> you knitted me together in my mother's womb.
> I praise you, for I am fearfully and wonderfully made.
> Wonderful are your works;
> my soul knows it very well.
> My frame was not hidden from you,
> when I was being made in secret,
> intricately woven in the depths of the earth.
> Your eyes saw my unformed substance;
> in your book were written, every one of them,
> the days that were formed for me,
> when as yet there was none of them.[65]

Jamie (Mom): For a while I operated in a fog and struggled with guilt. Lines of communication were severed and I felt like a failure as a mother. A breakthrough came when I apologized for my shortcomings. This went a long way toward reconciliation and effectively moving forward in adverse circumstances.

Jim (Dad): We understand that loving family members are sometimes absent in the life of pregnant teens. Fortunately, both families came together and stacked hands. We concluded that we would surround Brenna and Ryan with unconditional love, prayer, and support. We

---

[65]   Psalm 139:13–16

also reinstituted boundaries that would help them maintain discipline required to mature as adults and parents. Ultimately, their positive response to godly wisdom was a key ingredient to fruitful living.

Jamie (Mom): They wanted to get married, but we strongly encouraged deferring this major life decision. Although they assured us of their love, we told them self-sufficiency was required before we'd support a wedding.

Brock: It has always been easy for me to look on the bright side of things and tune out the negative. With that being said, it is often hard for me to reflect on the months leading up to the birth because I naturally try to forget all the bad. However, with it being such a long period of tension, I could only tune out so much.

The thing that I remember most as a sophomore in high school is just how confused I was. You could sense the tension in the room that morning in January when my brother and I were told that our sister had something to tell us. *Cool,* was my first thought when I heard she was pregnant, *I get to be an uncle.*

But then the crying, explaining, and arguments began and I had no idea what to think or feel. I tried to remain optimistic and to make everything okay, but I didn't know how. For about six months a prayer request in my small group was for peace and reconciliation in my family.

Eventually my optimism hit a breaking point. I was walking to class with two of my closest friends when I just stopped and started crying. They asked me what was wrong. "My family is falling apart," I said, "and I have no idea how to stop it." Without hesitation they both threw their arms around me and began to pray.

Jordan: I was in the eighth grade when Brenna became pregnant. I started to think more about my faith. I couldn't stop thinking about how this might change the family dynamics, which it did. This was the first major trial that I witnessed. During the next few months there was a lot of crying and arguing. At times Brock and I wouldn't come home to avoid hearing the latest fight. We'd go to a friend's house or to a local water tower that became an escape for us.

Around this time was when I discovered the power of prayer. I first thought I didn't want to talk to anyone about the situation, but I soon found myself praying and asking God for peace. During this time, I read Proverbs 3:5–6 many times and I tried to "trust in the Lord with all my heart."

Although it was difficult, I'm grateful for the experience. Living apart from God is harmful. I was more thankful to see the Lord rebuild our divided family. God's peace and patience prevailed and allowed us to focus on preparing for a baby. Initially, the pregnancy fractured us. But in the end it brought us much closer as a family.

Jamie (Mom): Afterward we realized that we somewhat abandoned the needs of our boys. We were so thankful people in ministry surrounded and encouraged them along the way.

Brenna: How are we doing? The simple version is that God's grace has sustained us. The complicated report is found in a series of events. Our parents have prayed over and supported us when we were still kids figuring it out. Siblings have been our best friends, babysitters, and soundboards through the roller-coaster life we've been living since then. Ryan and I have had peeks and valleys, but through biblical counsel from others, we are loving, communicating, and choosing to be there for one another through the wins and losses that come with being a spouse and parent.

Jim (Dad): Brenna and Ryan have now been married eight years. My granddaughter, Dakota, is nine, and is a sweetheart who loves to play games with "Mimi" and "Papa," and go for joy rides with me on the Harley. She has two younger brothers, Dax who is six, and Dawson who is three. Together as a family they are proving to be the exception to the statistics.

Brock: God in his perfect timing brought peace and reconciliation to our family. Not with just one, but three bundles of joy and a brother-in-law that I can't imagine living without.

And oh, yeah, the water tower; we each received a ticket for hanging out there. If you guessed that our already combustible law enforcement father chaffed about that, you'd be correct! So if you're looking for solitude, I'd recommend another location.

Jim (Dad): Yes, I confess I "chaffed." Can I get an "Amen" from a father out there?

The story is still being written as the journey continues. But we share *Our Family Was Pregnant* to offer hope that *exceptions* are possible. This circumstance, like all troubling times in life, required surrendering to God's sovereignty in order to restore unity in our family. It doesn't matter how we fail to measure up to God's design for our life, no situation is hopeless if you invite him into the mix!

LIGHT IN DARK PLACES

23

"Spiritual illumination will overcome shadows cast by sin."

A flashlight is an incredibly valuable tool for a peace officer. I carried one with me constantly regardless of the time of day or my specific assignment. While on patrol, and before flashlights were miniaturized, my Streamlight always rested between my legs on the driver's seat. This ensured it was never left behind when exiting the patrol unit.

Then Surefire and other brands miniaturized flashlights and equipped them with the same candela produced by the larger lights, and it was always on my duty belt. Finally, a light was developed and mounted to my Sig Sauer handgun. I was in illumination heaven!

A cop needs to have light available since it is not unusual to find yourself in dark places: a building search, homes with blacked out windows, darkened tunnels, etc....

Light is important because it defeats darkness every time! While light and dark are reality in the physical sense, they are also present spiritually.

A group of self-righteous men brought a woman caught in the darkness of adultery before Jesus. They reminded him that the Law of Moses commanded stoning. After a brief lesson, Jesus said to the woman, "[G]o, and from now on sin no more."[66] He then continued his public instruction, "I am the light of the world. Whoever follows me will not walk in darkness, but will have the light of life."[67]

Over a short period of time, our eyes will adjust to darkness to allow for *night vision*, but it's still dark. In a spiritual sense, some people constantly reside in dark places, so they do not see or appreciate the light. Their spiritual and moral eyesight has incrementally made the adjustments, and darkness is the new norm.

The apostle Paul wrote, "In their case, the god of this world has blinded the minds of the unbelievers, to keep them from seeing the light of the gospel of the glory of Christ, who is the image of God."[68]

Jesus further instructed his followers, "The light is among you for a little while longer. Walk while you have the light, lest darkness overtake you. The one who walks in the darkness does not know where he is going. While you have the light, believe in the light, that you may become sons of light."[69]

While physical light defeats darkness, spiritual illumination will overcome shadows cast by sin! If you have friends in dark places, be the light they need to see.

---

[66] John 8:11

[67] John 8:12

[68] 2 Corinthians 4:4

[69] John 12:35-37

JUSTIFIABLE HOMICIDE

24

"Just because we have a homicide does not mean a crime exists."

S ome in the Christian community want to apply "Thou shalt not kill"[70] as prohibitions for men and women who pursue a career in the military or law enforcement. After all, what happens when deadly force is required?

The Old Testament word used in Hebrew is *ratsach,* and was translated into the King James Version (KJV) as *kill.* But the Hebrew word has a much broader definition. Theologians, including those who compiled the commentary for the *Reformation Study Bible,* agree a more accurate translation is *murder.*[71] That is why the verse is translated, "You shall not murder" in the English Standard Version (ESV), New American Standard Version (NASB), New King James Version (NKJV), and the New Living Translation (NLT), among others.

---

[70] Exodus 20:13 and Deuteronomy 5:17 KJV

[71] https://www.biblegateway.com/resources/reformation-study-bible/Exod.20.13 – accessed on January 2, 2016.

Scenes that include death at the hands of another are labeled *homicides.* Just because we have a homicide does not mean a crime exists. Homicides can be categorized accidental, execution, justifiable, murder, and manslaughter. As you can see, some are criminal, others are not.

If a police officer takes the life of another using lawful force, it is deemed a justifiable homicide. (Determining what is lawful is not the topic of this section. But if you'd like to read my thoughts related to a controversial shooting, I commend to you the article, *Eye of the Storm.)*[72]

Justifiable homicide is not in conflict with the command in Exodus or Deuteronomy that says, "You shall not murder." If the actions are justified due to the perilous circumstances, it's not murder in the legal or biblical sense!

According to the Bible, the government has a responsibility to ensure the safety of its' citizenry and confront the wicked.

> For rulers are not a terror to good conduct, but to bad. Would you have no fear of the one who is in authority? Then do what is good, and you will receive his approval, for he is God's servant for your good. But if you do wrong, be afraid, for he does not bear the sword in vain. For he is the servant of God, an avenger who carries out God's wrath on the wrongdoer.[73]

This passage is foundational for peace officers and the military. As an extension of governing rulers, we are "God's servant for your good."

---

[72] http://www.lawenforcementtoday.com/2015/04/22/eye-of-the-storm/

[73] Romans 13:3,4

Understandably the question arises, "How can I adhere to a government that is in conflict with God's law, one that has forfeited righteous pursuits?" That is a great question.

I'm going to tackle a complex issue with a simple answer that may or may not be easily applied based upon specific circumstances. In the Introduction to this book, I quoted a passage from Timothy that is also appropriate here:

> First of all, then, I urge that supplications, prayers, intercessions, and thanksgivings be made for all people, for kings and all who are in high positions, that we may lead a peaceful and quiet life, godly and dignified in every way. This is good, and it is pleasing in the sight of God our Savior, who desires all people to be saved and to come to the knowledge of the truth. For there is one God, and there is one mediator between God and men, the man Christ Jesus, who gave himself as a ransom for all, which is the testimony given at the proper time.[74]

We are instructed to pray for our leaders as God created the institution of government for our good, not the other way around. We should pray for them regularly, whether we agree with their politics or not. But the government is run by the conscience of its' leaders to support a moral code. If their conscience has been corrupted, then it is no longer good and immorality will fill the void.

When leaders fail to be good, then a response might be in order because God cannot, and will not, bless sinful acts that enslave his people.

As Paul wrote to Timothy, "For there is one God, and there is one mediator between God and men, the man Christ Jesus...." The mediator is not government. As followers of Christ, we are to abide

---

[74] 1 Timothy 2:1–6

in him and obey God's commands. When in conflict, follow God's law. There might be negative consequences, but obedience is better than breaking fellowship with the Creator.

That is the simplified version to an extremely difficult topic. If you find yourself in an area of conflict, seek counsel in God's Word, ask for wisdom through prayer, and yield to the impressions of the Holy Spirit. Paul continued with counsel to Timothy:

> Have nothing to do with foolish, ignorant controversies; you know that they breed quarrels. And the Lord's servant must not be quarrelsome but kind to everyone, able to teach, patiently enduring evil, correcting his opponents with gentleness. God may perhaps grant them repentance leading to a knowledge of the truth, and they may come to their senses and escape from the snare of the devil, after being captured by him to do his will.[75]

There are those who've written extensively on the topic. David Hall's book, *Calvin in the Public Square: Liberal Democracies, Rights and Civil Liberties*, is a good resource. John Calvin was an esteemed theologian and pastor during the Protestant Reformation. Hall summarizes Calvin's basic view that all men are sinners, including kings and magistrates. God institutes government for the benevolent rule of people. When government doesn't measure up to this standard or becomes abusive and tyrannical, then others have the right to rebel according to predetermined guidelines.[76]

---

[75] 2 Timothy 2:23–26

[76] David W. Hall, *Calvin in the Public Square* (P&R Publishing 2009).

25

TELL THE TRUTH

"Once deception is unleashed, trust will vanish."

There is axiomatic humor that warns, "If you kill a bug, another thousand will come to the funeral." The same could be said for lying—tell one and it will require hoards more to cover your trail.

If I had to select a single virtue that would be the best place to begin curing social ills, it would be honesty. The personal and political agenda of many have led an overwhelming number of people down the road of deceit. Once deception is unleashed, trust will vanish. Many compromised business practices that lead to organizational failure are the result of lying. Unfortunately, *spin* is an accepted value if it helps the individual or group achieve a goal.

The Bible takes a straightforward stand on the issue. It is written, "You shall not bear false witness against your neighbor."[77] This is the ninth of the famous *Ten Commandments*, and Scripture takes a broad perspective on the term "neighbor."

Moses discusses witnesses and testifying against someone accused of a crime. "A single witness shall not suffice against a person for any

---

[77]   Exodus 20:16

crime...."[78] He continues, "The judges shall inquire diligently, and if the witness is a false witness and has accused his brother falsely, then you shall do to him as he had meant to do to his brother. So you shall purge the evil from your midst."[79]

The words "malicious" and "evil" are used to describe one bearing false witness against another. And the consequences were severe!

I was intentionally misled recurrently during the course of my career! Law enforcement officers are lied to with such impunity and frequency we jokingly tell career criminals we know they are lying because *their lips are moving*. Admittedly this is not very polite, but sometimes we need to find humor in the jungle of cynicism.

Jesus extolled unmerited graciousness for the corrupt as he was confident God's justice would trump human attempt at retaliation. Yet Christ upheld the virtue of honesty when He said, "Let what you say be simply 'Yes' or 'No'; anything more than this comes from evil."[80] In the context of Matthew 5, Jesus simply admonished others to *Tell the Truth*. It might be humbling, but it's not difficult.

---

[78] Deuteronomy 19:15
[79] Deuteronomy 19:18,19
[80] Matthew 5:37

26

GAUNTLET OF GOSSIP

"Wisdom provides details that heal, prudence withholds words that hurt."

Have you found yourself engaged in a conversation that had more variety than the gauntlet of gossip found in the magazine rack at the checkout counters, but delightfully continued anyway? The degrading information was just too juicy to hit the brakes, so you participated.

"Hey, did you hear what Brett did?"

"No, fill me in."

"He ... and then.... You should have seen the look on Kayla's face when she found out! Worse than that, Jen...."

"Unbelievable! I need to let Kayla's brother know. He is pretty tight with Jen and works in the bureau with her ex."

No doubt, you can fill in the salacious tidbits of hearsay. Cops are notorious for *gathering intel*. Even if it's of a personal nature. We have the uncanny ability to coax a friend or coworker out of information, just like we'd squeeze every detail out of a witness to a crime.

But when exercising this *gift* around the police department, it has been my experience that most of the conversations turn counterproductive—into rumors and gossip.

A colleague and I once discussed the volume of unproductive conversations that take place at the station. As a police manager I had to take action several times based upon malicious rumors that began in the hallways, at the water coolers, and on coffee breaks. Peers spreading personal information that maligned the reputation of another. Some of it true, much of it embellished, but most of it discussed to simply share "dirt."

We use the ten-code in Orange County, California. In our jurisdiction, the radio code "10-19" officially means, "Return or returning to station." At my department, as with many others, "10-19" morphed into, "At the station."

If "10-19" means "At the station" and gossip is prevalent within the walls of most police organizations (at least those I've visited), how ironic is it when I opened my Bible to Proverbs 10:19 and read, "When words are many, transgression is not lacking, but whoever restrains his lips is prudent." The New Living Translation is a little more blunt: "Too much talk leads to sin. Be sensible and keep your mouth shut."

Needless to say, the proverb from Solomon offers wise counsel to cops when they are 10-19—at the station.

Kurt Heinecke and Phil Vischer penned a song titled, *The Rumor Weed*. A small excerpt can amusingly help make my point:

> We've heard the one about Alfred
> It's strange, amazing, untrue
> But now that we've heard about Alfred
> We'd like to hear more about you...

[S]o what is a rumor?
It starts a story, maybe its true, maybe not
But once you repeat it, it's hard to defeat it
Now look at the mess that you've got.

I've also been engaged in ministry long enough to know that *prayer requests* can be disguised as gossip. So use caution in this area. The barometer I've tried to employ is simple. Wisdom provides details that heal, prudence withholds words that hurt. If my conversation does not help the situation or protect someone, then it is probably unnecessary. If it is unnecessary and contains a personal element, someone is likely being maligned in the *Gauntlet of Gossip*.

HE'S BEEN WITH JESUS

27

"Once Jesus transformed their lives, they were anything but normal.

Two things people avoid discussing in mixed company include religion and politics. Since I routinely proclaim the gospel of Christ to the law enforcement community and beyond, I have wondered if I'm viewed as a regular guy who is bold and strong, or a religious nut who is weak and foolish!

I enjoy riding motorcycles, many forms of exercise, shooting guns, and a wide variety of sports. Is the normalcy of these events discounted because of my spiritual faith? The reality is that I do not want to be identified as a *regular guy.*

Disciples John and Peter were fishermen by trade. Yet once Jesus transformed their lives they were anything but normal. In Acts 4 they were taken before "rulers and elders" and then questioned about their encounter that led to the healing of a crippled man. "Now when they saw the boldness of Peter and John and perceived that they were uneducated, common men, they were astonished. And they recognized that they had been with Jesus."[81]

---

[81]   Acts 4:13

After providing their story, the rulers realized the Galilean fishermen were different—"They had been with Jesus." They were not regular guys! And I do not want to be one either!

I hope others benefit from my written thoughts. But the reality is that God is busy working on me. I simply place some of the lessons that I've learned into written form.

To the surprise of some, I declare that I do not endorse ritualistic religion. According to the prophet Isaiah, "[R]ighteous deeds are like a polluted garment."[82] The NKJV says, "filthy rags."

Rather, I believe in a relationship with Jesus—one that saves my soul and causes good works as fruit of my faith. So whether I'm a religious nut or regular guy, the greatest compliment for me to hear is this: *"He's Been With Jesus."*

---

[82]   Isaiah 64:6

SECTION SIX
WITNESS STATEMENTS

REMEMBER MY CHAINS

28

"The cast iron links that restricted Paul's freedom were in place because he boldly proclaimed the gospel of Christ Jesus."

" Remember my chains. Grace be with you."[83] These were the words of the apostle Paul as he closed his letter to the Colossians while incarcerated in Rome.

Let the words "Remember my chains" resonate. They struck me with uniqueness as I read them recently. *What are my chains?* I inwardly wondered.

The cast-iron links that restricted Paul's freedom were in place because he boldly proclaimed the gospel of Christ Jesus. So again I ask, "What are my chains?"

If I'm honest, they include timidity, the desire to avoid awkward moments, insecurity due to lack of knowledge, and inconvenience among other reasons.

"Amazing grace," wrote John Newton, "that saved a wretch like me." Newton was the captain of a slave trade ship that saw all forms of inhumane treatment to living, breathing human beings during

---

[83] Colossians 4:18b

transport in the 1700s. Upon his conversion, he renounced the practice and entered ministry. "I once was lost, but now I'm found; was blind, but now I see," he expressed because God's grace rescued him.[84]

So now I discard my chains and proclaim for all to read that I follow Jesus as my Lord and Savior because his grace has found me, too.

Do not go into service another day without confident assurance that eternal life begins now, not the day your heart quits ticking. Jesus said, "Truly, truly, I say to you, whoever hears my word and believes him who sent me has eternal life. He does not come into judgment, but has passed from death to life."[85]

I have no chains or excuses. May God's grace be with you!

---

[84] http://www.anointedlinks.com/amazing_grace.html – accessed on January 4, 2016

[85] John 5:24

29

TOWN OF PHILIPPI

*"In defiance, they harmonized
'How Great Thou Art' for all to hear!"*

U nless you are well versed in history, you may be unfamiliar with King Philip II of Macedon, but he left a legacy. The town of Philippi was named after him, and his son was Alexander the Great.

When Paul and Silas visited Philippi on a missionary journey, a young slave girl who was possessed with a "spirit of divination" annoyingly stalked them for days. When they had enough of the taunting, they cast out the spirit. Interestingly enough, the owner of the slave was angry because she brought him a significant income through fortune-telling. When the spirit was excised, her powers were gone. The owner complained as if Paul and Silas had damaged his property, and false accusations were made. A mob formed and our missionaries were severely beaten and then jailed. In response to the unjustified punishment, Paul and Silas prayed and sang hymns.

While confined, there was an earthquake that opened the jail doors. Thinking they had escaped, the jailer planned to kill himself, fearing death to be an eventuality. "Do not harm yourself, for we are all here," Paul asserted. Amazed, the jailer repented and turned in faith to Christ.[86]

I've provided this abbreviated backstory because I believe it was on Paul's mind when he later wrote his letter to the Philippians. "Do nothing from rivalry or conceit, but in humility count others more significant than yourselves."[87] Did Paul and Silas demonstrate this kind of respectful deference to the guard? It's likely.

"So that at the name of Jesus every knee should bow, in heaven and on earth and under the earth, and every tongue confess that Jesus Christ is Lord, to the glory of God the Father."[88] You can include the jailer as one who made this confession of faith.

Think back to a time when you sustained a serious injury. Afterward, did you feel like singing and praying? Paul and Silas received "many blows" as they were "beaten with rods" before being locked up. Then in confinement, their feet were "fastened in stocks." Even with the abuse, they responded in song and prayer.

Christians across America are not yet being tortured for their faith, though the legal attacks are mounting. Last year I read a story about a high school band in Mississippi that was prohibited from playing, "How Great Thou Art" at the halftime show. This was the result of a lawsuit brought by a single student claiming discrimination, and the US District Court agreed with him. So the band was "benched."[89]

---

[86] Acts 16

[87] Philippians 2:3

[88] Philippians 2:10,11

[89] http://www.foxnews.com/opinion/2015/08/21/school-band-told-to-stop-performing-how-great-thou-art.html – accessed on January 4, 2016

The unjustified assault on Christian values continues. But I love the response of those in attendance at the football game. *They sang!* In defiance, they harmonized "How Great Thou Art" for all to hear! Perhaps they knew the story of Paul and Silas resorting to worship in song while being treated unjustly?

I don't know if the judge or the single plaintiff heard the response, but I have confidence that God will have the final word. "As I live, says the Lord, 'every knee shall bow to me, and every tongue shall confess to God.'"[90] Doesn't this passage sound similar to the earlier one from Philippians 2? I think Paul was serious.

Are you skeptical this will prove true? Then consider this: the *Encyclopedia of Biblical Prophecies* calculated that 27 percent of the entire Bible contains 1,817 predictive prophecies. This is true of no other book in the world, and it is a sure sign of its divine origin. Not one of these prophecies that has passed its time to be fulfilled has failed to be spot on.[91] That is what mathematicians call an anomaly, and that's why I'm confident that every judge, plaintiff, and others who defy God will ultimately confess that he is Lord!

Why is this necessary? Paul writes, "So then each of us will give an account of himself to God."[92]

Fram is a brand of after-market automotive parts. "You can pay me now, or pay me later," became their slogan. Enough said?

---

[90] Romans 14:11

[91] J. Barton Payne – *Encyclopedia of Biblical Prophecies* (Baker Book House Publishing, 1980), 674–75.

[92] Romans 14:12

ONE SENTENCE TESTIMONY

30

"God revealed his majesty to me when walking through the illness and death of my father."

When providing testimony in court, a witness is required to give direct answers to specific questions. An opposing attorney will challenge a free-flow narrative as *unresponsive* unless certain conditions are met.

Just like law enforcement professionals are called as witnesses in court, God has called followers of Christ to bear testimony as well. "But in your hearts honor Christ the Lord as holy, always being prepared to make a defense to anyone who asks you for a reason for the hope that is in you; yet do it with gentleness and respect."[93]

So why are so many Christians timid when expressing their spiritual view? Do we fear confrontation or losing a debate? Is panic present when discussing theology (the study of the nature of God and religious belief) or apologetics (reasoned arguments in justification of something)? Do we dread the question about hermeneutics (the interpretation of Scripture) or transliteration (the conversion of text from one script to another)?

---

[93]   1 Peter 3:15

Rest easy! God has aptly equipped men and women of faith with depth in these areas. Not that we shouldn't try to deepen our understanding. But for most, his instructions are simple. Provide the hope that is in you with gentleness and respect.

Perhaps you've heard it said that God has called us to be his witness, not his attorney. A witness merely provides a succinct one-sentence response. It is God's job to remove the spiritual veil of blindness.

"One thing I do know," said the man transformed by Jesus, "that though I was blind, now I see."[94] This individual was not attending Bible School, let alone possessing a graduate degree from seminary. He simply told his story!

Even Peter and John provided a succinct testimony incorporated into a longer dialogue when standing before the religious council. "Whether it is right in the sight of God to listen to you rather than to God you must judge, for we cannot but speak of what we have seen and heard."[95]

God has called me to provide an in-depth testimony at various times before attentive audiences. But he has called me with far greater frequency to provide a *one-sentence testimony* in response to various questions in the neighborhood, workplace, and other venues.

➤ "My relationship with God changed when he salvaged my marriage."
➤ "God revealed his majesty to me when walking through the illness and death of my father."
➤ "I am woefully insufficient without the help of Christ."

---

[94] John 9:25

[95] Acts 4:19

➢ "It is in the 'white water' of life that my faith is tested to be true."

➢ "The act of baptism represents dying with Jesus and then being raised to a new life in Christ."

➢ "I was in agony living for myself, but fulfilled as I follow Jesus."

Each statement of fact was delivered in response to a question. A witness is not expected to provide all the answers, and neither are you. Do your best to acquire wisdom and knowledge, but simply tell what you know to be true in a spirit of love. What is your *One Sentence Testimony*?

SECTION SEVEN
PAIN AND SUFFERING

31

DIVINE DISRUPTION

"God's plans frequently interrupt my comfort and convenience, but I benefit nonetheless."

I have often used the term *divine appointments* when referring to circumstances that God has placed me in while ministering to others. I have learned that God affirms me more than I assist others when he strategically places me in this way. A friend used the term *divine disruptions* when referring to these encounters. Once I considered his wisdom, I couldn't agree more. God's plans frequently interrupt my comfort and convenience, but I benefit nonetheless.

Whether these are appointments or disruptions, God divinely places us in opportunities to proclaim the good news. At times God can actually design the calamity, creating a prospect to minister to others who might otherwise miss the heaven-sent information. If you doubt this, simply look at Jonah's circumstances. God told Jonah, "Arise, go to Nineveh, that great city, and call out against it, for their evil has come up before me."[96]

Jonah didn't like the Ninevites, so he fled to Tarshish aboard a ship. Yet God divinely disrupted Jonah's journey:

---

[96] Jonah 1:2

➢ "But the Lord hurled a great wind upon the sea...."[97]

➢ "So they cast lots, and the lot fell on Jonah."[98]

➢ "So they picked up Jonah and hurled him into the sea."[99]

➢ "And the Lord appointed a great fish to swallow Jonah."[100]

➢ "And the Lord spoke to the fish, and it vomited Jonah out upon dry land."[101]

Finally, Jonah yielded to God's call and brought the message to those in Nineveh. Unbelievably, after seeing their favorable response, Jonah continued in willful obstinance. Again, God created distress to get his attention:

➢ "Now the Lord God appointed a plant and made it come over Jonah, that it might be a shade over his head, to save him from discomfort. So Jonah was exceedingly glad because of the plant."[102]

➢ "But when dawn came up the next day, God appointed a worm that attacked the plant, so that it withered."[103]

➢ "When the sun arose, God appointed a scorching east wind and the sun beat down on Jonah so that he was faint."[104]

---

[97]   Jonah 1:4

[98]   Jonah 1:7b

[99]   Jonah 1:15

[100]   Jonah 1:17

[101]   Jonah 2:10

[102]   Jonah 4:6

[103]   Jonah 4:7

[104]   Jonah 4:8a

The prophet Isaiah knew the reality of God's authority well when he shared words from the Almighty. "I form light and create darkness, I make well-being and create calamity, I am the Lord who does all these things."[105]

Do not mistake calamity with temptation to sin. "Let no one say when he is tempted, 'I am being tempted by God,' for God cannot be tempted with evil, and he himself tempts no one."[106]

God did not provide Jonah with the temptation to sin by running from him, but he certainly designed cataclysmic circumstances to get Jonah's attention.

Disrupting comfort might be God's way to get our attention too! This is when we must learn complete reliance, not square off against him. If we choose bitterness, be prepared. The shade might *wither* and the *scorching wind and sun* might be required to make us *tap out*.

Perhaps this is a difficult message to read. Maybe you view God as a *bully*, imposing his will on poor Jonah, or even us. Conversely, I imagine there are some people from Nineveh who would provide a sense of gratitude, and we all have Ninevites in our life who might benefit from a *Divine Disruption*!

---

[105] Isaiah 45:7

[106] James 1:13

32

GUILT AND REMORSE

"We cannot change the past, but we can alter our future based upon our reaction to that which has devastated us."

P eace officers routinely become involved in activity that can lead to guilt and remorse. The high-risk nature of the business demands instantaneous decisions that do not always turn out so well. When the circumstances are grave, the side effects can be disabling. These emotional expressions can lead one to believe the fetal position is the best option.

Peter suffered through guilt and remorse after he denied Jesus— not once or twice, but three times. To exacerbate the anguish, Jesus predicted his denial to which Peter stridently claimed would never happen. Once Jesus' prophetic utterance came true, Matthew wrote, "And he (Peter) went out and wept bitterly."[107] Have you been there?

The good news is that God offers salvation through his Son, Jesus, and redemption for us by obedience to his Word. When Jesus met Peter after the resurrection, he asked him three times if he loved him. On each occasion Peter affirmed his devotion to his Lord and Savior,

---

[107]   Matthew 26:75b

and Jesus successively instructed Peter, "Feed my lambs," "Tend my sheep," and "Feed my sheep."[108] Jesus continued by foretelling Peter's future and completed his directions by saying, "Follow me."[109]

Pain and suffering from guilt and remorse are real. We cannot change the past, but we can alter our future based upon our reaction to that which has devastated us. While the healing process is a journey, there are basic steps that need to be taken. *Confessing trespasses, forgiving others,* and *following Jesus* are the beginning to a stable foundation. We are unable to demand forgiveness from those who've wounded us, but the counsel from Paul will bring healing. "If possible, so far as it depends on you, live peaceably with all."[110]

---

[108] John 21:15–17

[109] John 21:19b

[110] Romans 12:18

33

MUDDY WATER

"Until you die to yourself in this life, you will not see the majesty of heaven in eternity."

Every time we lose a courageous man or woman serving in the military or law enforcement, it is usually a premature, job-related death. As such, it is important to look at the deeper meaning of life.

Wounded warrior advocate and country music performer Trace Adkins sings a tune about being baptized.

[I]t's a long way from where I've been back to my hometown

> But there's a man in me I need to drown
> Baptize me in that muddy water
> Wash me clean in amazing grace
> I ain't been living like I oughta....

The lyricist was writing scriptural truth!

There are roughly twenty-two verses that discuss dying to yourself so you can be alive in Christ. Two of my favorites are found in a letter from the apostle Paul to the Galatians. "I have been crucified with Christ. It is no longer I who live, but Christ who lives in me. And the life I now live in the flesh I live by faith in the Son of God, who loved me and gave himself for me."[111] He continued the theme later in the same letter. "And those who belong to Christ Jesus have crucified the flesh with its passions and desires."[112]

Baptism is not an act that assures salvation—eternity with God in heaven. Rather, it is an act of obedience. Jesus said, "Go therefore and make disciples of all the nations, baptizing them in the name of the Father and of the Son and of the Holy Spirit, teaching them to observe all things that I have commanded you."[113]

The act of baptism represents dying with Jesus and then being raised to a new life in Christ, "For when you were baptized, you were buried with Christ, and in baptism you were also raised with Christ."[114]

Luke, the physician, wrote in his gospel, "And he (Jesus) said to all, 'If anyone would come after me, let him deny himself and take up his cross daily and follow me.'"[115]

"Now if we have died with Christ," wrote Paul to the Romans, "we believe that we shall also live with him."[116]

It is not easy to deal with death. But until you die to yourself in this life, you will not see the majesty of heaven in eternity. So if you've wondered what your purpose in life should be, it's to live for Christ by dying to yourself. Everything else takes a back seat.

---

[111] Galatians 2:20

[112] Galatians 5:24

[113] Matthew 28:19–20

[114] Colossians 2:12

[115] Luke 2:23

[116] Romans 6:8

34

SCARS OF REMEMBRANCE

"While my body is repaired, the scar will remind me of the damage that was done."

I have a seven-inch surgical scar on my right knee. While it's healed and my leg functions fine, it reminds me of past trauma and the road well-traveled.

Rewind to 1987. My leg was twisted and churned during a rollover accident. I had so many injuries the damage to my knee went undiagnosed by questionable medical practices as I lay in a hospital bed. It remained that way even as I went home to heal after a few weeks.

It was not until I returned to work four months later and gave chase to a strong-armed robbery suspect that my knee buckled and I hit the ground writhing in pain. A torn MCL took me to my first arthroscopic surgery. Because I was young and invincible, or so I thought, I ignored the medical advice by continuing physical activity that eventually led to the erosion of inner parts holding the joint together.

In 2007 I had a second arthroscopy to clear the damage. The orthopedic specialist said it was simply a matter of time before the knee would fail to function and I would need an artificial joint.

By 2013 the cartilage was gone, the meniscus was sanded away, bones rubbing together developed a spur on the inner knee, and the MCL, ACL, and PCL's all looked like "shredded drapes" according to my surgeon.

"Tell me something I don't already know" was my reply.

"Okay, your leg is about 20 degrees off-axis. Can you see how it bows outward from the knee down? That's not an illusion. It is because the bone spur is so large it has created a wedge forcing your leg in the wrong direction." So it was time for my third surgery—complete knee replacement.

My new joint consists of titanium and polyethylene. It is secured in place beneath the surgical scar. My leg is no longer off-axis, but straight.

While my body is repaired, the scar will remind me of the damage that was done. It's unfortunate, but I cannot undo the past or wallow in the present.

We all have scars. Some are physical, some emotional. God is in the business of healing wounds, but he will not impose his will upon us. We need to accept him as the Great Physician and fully understand his eternal perspective for our wellbeing is always spiritual healing, but may or may not include physical healing.

Two people who've demonstrated incredible faith and prayed for physical healing include Joni Eareckson Tada and Nick Vujicic. Joni became a quadriplegic following a diving accident as a teenager. Nick was born without arms and legs. Each had traumatic emotional and physical scars, but they've experienced spiritual healing and have been instruments for God in ways that are too wonderful for words—

opportunities that would be lost if they clung to anger, bitterness, or resentment.

Joni's ministry[117] and Nick's outreach[118] bring inspiration and hope. They each understand that physical healing does not always lead to spiritual healing, but spiritual healing will lead to physical healing in eternity since it is written, "So it is with the resurrection of the dead. What is sown is perishable; what is raised is imperishable. It is sown in dishonor; it is raised a spiritual body. If there is a natural body, there is also a spiritual body."[119]

"But our citizenship is in heaven and from it we await a Savior, the Lord Jesus Christ, who will transform our lowly body to be like his glorious body, by the power that enables him even to subject all things to himself."[120]

That is powerful stuff! But did you really grasp it? Our lowly (broken, mutilated, deformed, disfigured, burned, or simply aged) body to be like his glorious (perfect, complete, illuminating, magnificent, and ageless) body!

This is where healing begins. "[I]f you confess with your mouth that Jesus is Lord and believe in your heart that God raised him from the dead, you will be saved."[121]

After that it is a series of decisions that reinforce daily renewal in your commitment. Jesus said, "Whoever loves his life loses it, and whoever hates his life in this world will keep it for eternal life. If

---

[117]   http://www.joniandfriends.org

[118]   http://www.lifewithoutlimbs.org

[119]   1 Corinthians 15:42–44

[120]   Philippians 3:20–21

[121]   Romans 10:9

anyone serves me, he must follow me; and where I am, there will my servant be also. If anyone serves me, the Father will honor him."[122]

Jesus is waiting in the symbolic emergency room of life. If you surrender your life to him, your imperfect, perishable body will be made glorious and imperishable in eternity. Are you ready to be healed?

---

[122] John 12:25,26

SECTION EIGHT
BACKUP SUPPORT

35

BEING BARNABAS

*"Engage truth and ensure that your words,
thoughts, and actions are integrated with his
instruction."*

Think about those in your life who zap your strength. It is likely you've never heard a favorable word from their lips. Likewise, those you enjoy being around breath life into you with refreshing conversations and words that provide confidence and cheer.

Providing encouragement will relay energy to the recipient. Receiving affirmation will put a skip in your step. It is important to give and receive each one as part of the mutually beneficial social construct in which we exist.

That is why Barnabas was vitally important to the early church. His real name was Joseph, but they called him Barnabas because it means "son of encouragement." He mentored and encouraged Paul after his conversion, and was instrumental in connecting Paul to the rest of the apostles, helping facilitate what had previously been a stormy relationship. Paul in turn mentored many others, and of course went on to write most of the New Testament.

Barnabas also mentored and encouraged John Mark who wrote the gospel of Mark. While Barnabas did not author any books in the Bible (unless you consider the slim chance he is the unknown author of Hebrews), you can be sure that his fingerprints are all over the pages of Scripture.

I hope my encouragement comes across loud and clear to those who carry a shield. Peace officers are an ambassador with a badge representing the agency for which they are employed. They were chosen to wear the uniform. I hope each one does so with humility and pride. There are no routine traffic stops, alarm calls, crime reports, or arrest scenarios. That is why they wear body armor and carry a firearm.

If you are the loved one, I simply give thanks for sacrificing your *normal* life for the bizarre and unpredictable nature of law enforcement.

For the peace officer, there is no doubt that you will experience uncertainty every day in one way or another. Prayer is vital. Express your love and adoration for God's creation. Implore his help to flee from every form of manipulation and temptation. Engage truth and ensure that your words, thoughts, and actions are integrated with his instruction.

A lack of integration leads to disconnection. A trailer disconnected from a truck will veer off course and crash. Humanity is no different when separated from God.

May we all be Barnabas to someone today!

DOSE OF ENCOURAGEMENT

36

"Use the spiritual gifts that God has given you and the deposits you make into your world will multiply."

M any years ago when my sons left for college, we gathered close friends, small group leaders, and youth pastors who influenced their life during the formative years. It was a time of affirmation and encouragement. Naturally, as their father, I felt the obligation to send them away with something of value. I provided them with the following charge. My goal was to reinforce their development as godly men. I offer a *Dose of Encouragement* hoping to hearten your resolve in whatever you face today:

> My little boys no longer, but young men you've become. As you gain knowledge, may you find intelligence. As you gain understanding, may you obtain wisdom. As you pursue godly obedience, may you become more useful for his kingdom. Combine all three elements and you become a useful, wise, intelligent man full of character for our culture, comfort for humanity, competent in your craft, and like Christ in every way.
>
> Wherever you walk there will be an effect. May the useful, wise, and intelligent men you become influence the effect of your steps.

Follow where you must but lead where you can. The world is filled with drifters and people who masquerade as leaders, but their compass is off course. Their decisions lead to chaos and remorse. You cannot always lead from the front but you can provide influence wherever you are placed. Influence is earned by investing in others.

Use the spiritual gifts that God has given you and the deposits you make into your world will multiply. Be men of courage, remembering that courage is not the absence of fear, but the presence of mind to act in pursuit of truth and righteousness despite your fear.

As you strive to become the men I've described, throw pride to the side and humble yourself in favor of the Lord. Cast your every care upon him for he cares for you. Seek his ways and he will give you the desires of your heart. Fill your heart and your mind with the values of the Lord and he will fill your sail to capacity.

There is no denying that you will experience doubt every day in one way or another. When in doubt, pray. As you pray, spray to all fields. Express your love and adoration for his creation. Implore his help to flee from every form of manipulation and temptation. Engage the Scriptures and pray that your words, thoughts, and actions will be integrated with his instruction.

You are my sons and I am proud of you. Always express love for your mother and cherish your sister and her husband. Remember, you are mentors to their children. Assume the responsibility with a sense of faithfulness. Prepare yourselves for your future brides as gentlemen who honor their beauty and gender. Keep a watchful eye on your cousins walking the educational path with you. Have their backs and enjoy the journey together. Encourage and support them. Love and laugh with them as loved ones. The experiences together will create a bond and connection that will sustain you through many of life's trials.

Be a beacon to the lost, a watchtower to the faithful, and a friend to all. Be shrewd as a serpent yet innocent as a dove. Be the gatekeeper in your world, cautious about what is allowed into the inner sanctum. You are part of the world but set apart for holiness. Love godliness and hate sin. Walk in the Spirit and steer clear of the flesh. Refuel in the Word daily, put on the full armor of God, and live for an audience of one, your Father in heaven. Go with God and go with my blessing for you are my beloved sons.

SECTION NINE
HUMOR LEADING TO TRUTH

CHARACTERS IN THE GYM

37

"How you react to others in the body of Christ is a reflection on the depth of your faith."

Exercise has been prevalent in my life. Being a cop has something to do with it, but I've always gravitated toward sports. As a result, I've worked out in dozens of gyms over the years.

I've taken note of different *characters* that rotate from station to station in various fitness centers. They include:

➢ Steroid Dude – The one whose nonverbal communication says, "Get out of my way."
➢ Meathead – This guy flexes while he walks in an effort to prove he's super developed, yet his physique does not match his gait.
➢ The Certified Fitness Trainer – She motivates correct form on every movement.
➢ Forest Gump – The one running like a robot on the treadmill when you arrive, and still maintaining the same pace one or two hours later when you leave.

- Mr. Has Been – Unbearably he's still wearing his high school gym shorts, just slightly out of date.
- The Jug-Carrying Water Guzzler – His clear, one-gallon milk carton is filled with water, and he's usually drinking from it between sets.
- The Knit Cap Heavy Metal Man – He's rock solid and looks like he plays the drums for a heavy metal band or got "yoked" serving time in prison.
- Ms. Botox, Breast Augmentation Woman – Her oversized body parts in undersized outfits frequently break the concentration of everyone around.
- Captain America – This guy looks like he just graduated from one of the military service academies, and you're glad he's on our side.
- The Troller – The gym is an extension of the local bar for this person looking for a date. Flirting takes priority over exercise.
- Dodgeball Guy – Think of Ben Stiller in the movie by the same name. He is a combination of the Troller, Mr. Has Been, and Meathead.

The gym is a place filled with like-minded people regarding health, but it's also complete with an unwritten and erroneous *pecking order,* placing the strong and fit at the upper scale.

The church can be much the same way. I will not list a group of characters, but you probably know what I mean. As a result, there can be *preferred people* there as well. The knowledgeable, attractive, and wealthy tend to represent the *upper crust.*

My point is that it ought not be! And the spiritual deficiency goes well beyond the walls of the church.

Before Willie Lyle was installed as pastor at the Sango United Methodist Church in Clarksville, Tennessee, he lived on the streets for five days. This was not a social experiment, but a response to a call from God in order to gain a perspective previously unattained, and required to minister with a newfound compassion.

Flushing himself of the luxuries in life, Lyle quickly discovered the disrespect and disdain that can find one who is viewed as a vagabond. "Generally speaking, people are not kind to the homeless," he observed. "I know there are people who live on the street and choose to do so. I am talking about the homeless and poor who find themselves in circumstances beyond their control, and they have nothing," he explained. "Sadly, sometimes they don't even have hope. They most definitely want food and shelter, but they also seek the food and shelter found in the message of Christ."[123]

Lyle experienced a program called the Food Initiative where he met some people who knew how to minister to others. "These two high school boys called me 'sir,' introduced themselves to me, shook my hand, and wanted to know how I was doing. They treated me with respect and dignity.... Each had a servant attitude, not a judgmental (one)."[124]

Lyle discovered, "Too many of us only want to serve God one hour each week. That doesn't cut it. That is not God's plan."[125]

He chose a unique method to deliver his first message before the new congregation. "While he preached, his daughter-in-law cut his hair and his daughter helped shave off his scruffy beard. He changed

---

[123]   http://www.theleafchronicle.com/article/20130628/NEWS01
        /306280035?nclick_check=1 – accessed on January 1, 2016

[124]   Ibid

[125]   Ibid

shoes, and beneath the overcoat he was wearing his Sunday clothes. He put on a tie and his suit coat, all the while continuing to preach his message. "Before the 200 people gathered that morning, he went from looking like a homeless person to the new pastor of the congregation," reported Tim Parrish for *The Leaf Chronicle*.[126] "You see, we look at the outside of others and make judgments. God looks inside at our heart and sees the truth."[127]

"This was not some grandstand show on my part. I wanted everybody to know what I had been through, what I had learned, and the physical and emotional discomfort I experienced that I am still dealing with. And I made sure to mention more than once that Christ was not comfortable on the cross."[128]

Most serving in law enforcement have routinely witnessed the vices that cause many to become destitute, whether from drugs, alcohol, or gambling addictions. Peace officers have also been challenged finding solutions for the mentally ill who cross our path. These problems are real, and law enforcement is trying to find remedies. The church is also on the front lines, as it should be. As a result, our worship centers and sanctuaries will have some of "the least of these" in our presence.

I am not using Lyle's experiences to excuse willful acts of rebellion that lead to negative consequences. Nor is this a message encouraging aid to the con artists, or professional beggars who choose to leach off the generosity of others in direct conflict with the biblical prescription. But it's my goal to challenge each one of us to examine our hearts and align them with God's. Are we able to see

---

[126] Ibid

[127] Ibid

[128] Ibid

through our preconceived biases and work toward unity in Christ regardless of social status, race, gender, or even church affiliation?

"For in Christ Jesus you are all sons of God, through faith. For as many of you as were baptized into Christ have put on Christ. There is neither Jew nor Greek, there is neither slave nor free, there is no male and female, for you are all one in Christ Jesus. And if you are Christ's, then you are Abraham's offspring, heirs according to promise."[129]

While there are different roles for people in the church, there are no preferences regarding one above another. How you react to others in the body of Christ is a reflection on the depth of your faith.

---

[129] Galatians 3:26–29

CAUGHT IN THE SNARE

38

*"Playing my role to the hilt,
his story fell on a heart of stone."*

S taging a vehicle burglary on a new officer's police unit is a staple in the arsenal of pranks at our department. But when the officer doesn't realize he's been *punked, duped, pranked,* or whatever term you'd like to use, it takes humor to a new level.

On a relatively calm Saturday morning, I received a radio transmission from *Newbie.* "Sergeant, can you come over here? I have a little problem." He just cleared an audible alarm call and was parked at the backside of a shopping center.

"En route," I replied.

"Hey, boss," chimed in *Old Salt* on an alternate radio frequency, "I'll see what he needs."

I was immediately suspicious, since *Old Salt* rarely volunteered to assist new officers with trivial problems. To confirm my suspicions, *Old Salt* told me, "He's in a pretty bad area. Maybe his unit was 'window smashed' while he was checking the audible."

"Copy that. If so, have him report to me at the station," I affirmed as I decided to play along.

Old Salt arrived at *Newbie's* location, feigning disgust at the shards of broken safety glass inside the passenger door of the new officer's patrol unit. *Newbie* brokenheartedly voiced, "They took all my gear! Everything is gone."

Since *Old Salt* staged the crime by rolling down the passenger window, spread broken glass on the interior of the police unit, and temporarily heisted *Newbie's* gear, he relayed rather stoically, "You're lucky. At least they didn't get the shotgun out of the mount."

"What should I do?" said a distraught *rookie*.

"Check the rooftops, trash dumpsters, and every nook and cranny behind the businesses for remnants of your stuff," exhorted *Old Salt*. "I'll dust the door for prints."

Thirty minutes later *Newbie* was aghast at the predicament. Upon returning to his unit, and failing to notice the *wily veteran* had not lifted a finger looking for latent prints, he asked for instructions.

"Get to the station and report it to *Sarge*," barked *Old Salt*. "He's not gonna be happy."

When the young buck arrived at the department, he told me about his victimization. He carried on by saying the experience would make him a much better police officer in the future.

Playing my role to the hilt, his story fell on a heart of stone. "Is that right? Well, put your value lesson on hold. Confirm you let someone break into *my* police unit? They shattered a window and stole your gear? Who cares about your gear—what about *my* police car?" I bellowed, holding fast in character.

"I'll replace the window, Sergeant. I'm really sorry."

In the meantime, I instructed *Old Salt* and his co-conspirators to clean the glass out of *Newbie's* car, rollup the window, and return his gear to the passenger compartment.

Once the vandals surreptitiously made their crime disappear, I told *Newbie* to retrieve the VIN and license plate number from his unit. Each would be needed for the crime report. He dejectedly walked to the parking garage. As he approached the car, he noticed his gear was in place, but apparently failed to realize the window was "repaired."

At this point, most who've been duped usually realize it—but not this guy. On video we have him kicking up his heels, saying, "Yippee! Oh, happy day!" I kid you not!

I can't believe we hired such a gullible soul, were my thoughts.

Newbie returned to my office to exclaim the terrific news. "Sergeant, you're not going to believe it! My gear has been returned! Everything! It's all there!" He was so happy I felt guilty for a split second as I remained the stern disciplinary.

"You don't say! Well, good for you! What about the window? Did it get 'returned' too?" I asked.

With a lengthy pause and quizzical look on his face, he finally said, "Wow, I didn't notice. I'll go look."

Now I'm really getting worried. He's easy to fool, *and* his powers of observation are lacking!

The fleecing continued as we shattered his innocence. With the hidden video camera still rolling, *Newbie* returned to his police car to discover the window was intact. "It doesn't get better than this!" he howled.

Everyone in the building was privately snickering as *Newbie* returned to my office. "You're not going to believe it, Sergeant, but my window is fine!"

"Son, did you ever consider that you're getting punked?" I finally asked.

The light came on. His eyes rolled heavenward and a smile stretched across his face as he affirmed, "Oh, they got me! They got me real good!"

Indeed they did. *Newbie* went on to become a fine officer once his naivety was broken, and *Old Salt* developed more creative ways to make "new boots" believe they had been victimized.

One purpose for this chapter is to help you laugh. As Solomon said, "A joyful heart is good medicine...."[130] But the greater reason is to illustrate a biblical truth. Just as *Newbie* was deceived, Satan deceives people regularly. There are thirty-five places in Scripture that discuss this kind of deception. Here are two worth noting.

> And the Lord's servant must not be quarrelsome but kind to everyone, able to teach, patiently enduring evil, correcting his opponents with gentleness. God may perhaps grant them repentance leading to a knowledge of the truth, and they may come to their senses and escape from the snare of the devil, after being captured by him to do his will.[131]

> And even if our gospel is veiled, it is veiled to those who are perishing. In their case the god of this world has blinded the minds of the unbelievers, to keep them from seeing the light of the gospel of the glory of Christ, who is the image of God.[132]

In the story, *Old Salt* used cunning, yet believable measures to deceive. The truth was veiled from *Newbie*. His mind had formed an incorrect conclusion based upon the deception. It could not be

---

[130] Proverbs 17:22a

[131] 2 Timothy 2:24–26

[132] 2 Corinthians 4:3,4

altered, regardless of the fluid nature of the joke. Finally, *Newbie* saw the light and discovered he had been snared by *Old Salt.*

The truth is simple and succinct. Living in the light of God's Word, my friends, will help you avoid getting *Caught in the Snare.*

THE PROGRESSIVE TEN COMMANDMENTS

39

"To cast the Ten Commandments aside as insignificant demonstrates historical ignorance, spiritual isolation, and is a conceptual catastrophe to the good order of civilization."

W e've all read story after story outlining lawsuits filed by self-proclaimed *progressives*. Disguised as *tolerance* and *anti-discrimination*, their goals are to coerce and eliminate faith-based institutions (primarily Christianity) from hearkening a voice or displaying symbols anywhere open to public view.

Since one of the objects of continued attack includes the *Ten Commandments*, I believe they would like to erase them altogether, or at the very least, amend each one to fit their way of thinking.

I've done just that—amended the God-ordained words inscribed by Moses to fit their platform. I'd like to think I was creative in doing so, but the sad reality is this fits the chorus we hear all too frequently.

1. **You shall have no other gods before me** … with government being the one exception.

2. **You shall not make idols**...but ideology that is anti-God is encouraged.

3. **You shall not take the name of the Lord your God in vain**...because we're making it illegal to use his name anywhere outside of a house of worship.

4. **Remember the Sabbath day, to keep it holy**...but feel free to pursue other idols that you view as worthy competition. (Furthermore, expect to lose Christian-related holidays, like Thanksgiving, Christmas, and Easter from the public calendar. Eventually we'll discontinue using the word "holiday" altogether, since it derived from the words "holy" and "day.")

5. **Honor your father and your mother**...as long as they adhere to the progressive movement. If not, discard them as irrelevant to modern culture.

6. **You shall not murder**...except in the case of an unborn child. But never refer to it as a baby. *Fetus* is the accepted term until detached from its' mother's womb.

7. **You shall not commit adultery**...unless you're simply following your heart because it feels like the right thing to do.

8. **You shall not steal**...we'll simply label it a new tax or government fee.

9. **You shall not bear false witness**...unless it furthers our ideology or sways the elective process.

10. **You shall not covet**...we crave your earnings and will redistribute them to ourselves first, our power base second, and anything but edifying causes third.

May the original *Ten Commandments*[133] prevail as foundational to all laws that govern our nation since the giver declared, "'I am the

---

[133] Exodus 20:3–17 and Deuteronomy 5:7–21

Lord your God, who brought you out of the land of Egypt, out of the house of slavery."[134]

To cast them aside as insignificant demonstrates historical ignorance, spiritual isolation, and is a conceptual catastrophe to the good order of civilization.

After writing this chapter, I feel compelled to pray. If you are in agreement with me, I ask that you pray along.

> Lord, please forgive me for using the sacredness of your inspired words in satire. Fortunately, you know my heart and the driving force that motivates my writing, and it's to trust and obey each inerrant word in Scripture. Even those deemed outdated by any movement attempting to alter your truth to fit the desires of our flesh.
>
> Help me to obey government demands until I'm asked to violate your holy ordinance. If that occurs, give me wisdom and courage to proceed in a manner consistent with your instruction. I ask that you draw our leaders to repentance in faith for salvation, and call upon your name for wise counsel. In the name of Jesus I pray, amen.

---

[134]   Exodus 20:2 and Deuteronomy 5:6

40

YOU MIGHT BE A COP IF...

"You refuse to sit with your back to the door at a restaurant, even while off duty."

In the spirit of Jeff Foxworthy's *You Might Be a Redneck* shtick, here we find facts that are somewhat unique to law enforcement officers. These items are not meant to be funny, they are simply indicative that *"You Might Be a Cop If..."*

➢ You drive with the window down while your heater or air conditioner is on.

➢ You say "Good morning" when arriving for work at 2200 hours.

➢ You say "Good night" when leaving work at 0700 hours.

➢ Along with the lint in your pocket is ammunition left over from range qualification.

➢ You refuse to sit with your back to the door at a restaurant, even while off duty.

➢ You categorize other patrons as you size them up.

➢ You take notes on the back of your hand.

➢ You are on a first name basis with the clerk at 7-11 since you visit every night for a cup of coffee.
➢ You cover the peephole while standing off center when knocking on a door—on and off duty.
➢ You hold your flashlight in your armpit more than your hand.
➢ You're the first to criticize the foolishness of another while also being readily available to help with their distress.
➢ You equate the sound of Velcro with *tactics* and *officer safety*.
➢ The sound of clicking handcuffs gets your adrenaline pumping in a purely professional way.
➢ You place a spare flashlight everywhere in your house and automobile.
➢ Your *Extreme Ops* pocketknife is with you at all times.
➢ A *keeper* is not the date you bring home to meet your mother, but the way your gun belt remains in place.
➢ You've *cleared* your own home simply because something seemed out of place.
➢ You complete sentences for your partner because you've spent so many hours working together.
➢ *Controller* is not something used for a video game, it's something that you are!
➢ You discuss the nomenclature of a firearm like a coach will converse about a playbook.
➢ Your locker room discussions are as morbid as a horror movie, but the details are based upon your professional experience.

I'm trying to use fun facts to make a point. Peace officers, like many vocations, develop characteristics that are unique to the performance of their duty. They are created in the likeness of others who've gone before and serve beside them. We laugh about it but accept it as true.

Purposefully, our Heavenly Father did much the same thing. "So God created man in his own image, in the image of God he created him; male and female he created them."[135]

We shouldn't be surprised when comradery develops so quickly working alongside others who are likeminded and engaging adversaries. It is how God wired us. The same thing happens when we yield our life to Christ. "But he who is joined to the Lord becomes one spirit with him."[136]

Adding to the common bond shared by cops is oftentimes feeling misunderstood by critics who have not walked in our footsteps. *They do not know that which created us—a sum total of our training and experience—so how can they criticize?*

This feeling of isolation is not unique to peace officers. Many people feel the same loneliness.

In faithfulness to his children, God understands.

> See what kind of love the Father has given to us, that we should be called children of God; and so we are. The reason why the world does not know us is that it did not know him. Beloved, we are God's children now, and what we will be has not yet appeared; but we know that when he appears we shall be like him, because we shall see him as he is. And everyone who thus hopes in him purifies himself as he is pure.[137]

When I was young and immature, I was rarely told that I looked like my dad. Now as a mature, middle-aged man, with features

---

[135]   Genesis 1:27

[136]   1 Corinthians 6:17

[137]   1 John 3:1–3

aging daily, I frequently hear that I resemble my late father. What an honor to be told that I bear a resemblance to a man whose focus was continually on the Lord. I live to have my heart beat as his did, to be a God-centered, devoted follower of Christ, living in the Spirit for God's glory.

You might be a cop if you do the things listed earlier in this chapter, but "Whoever says he abides in him ought to walk in the same way in which he walked."[138]

---

[138] 1 John 2:6

41

MY SUBTLE
SOLILOQUY

*"As a youngster I wanted to **Get Smart** as*
***Adam 12** inspired me."*

T he public has always been obsessed with police work. As a
result, the entertainment industry has taken television viewers
from the *Southland* of Los Angeles to *Chicago P.D.* and further east
to *NYPD Blue*. Crime was solved on *The Streets of San Francisco,* with
Miami Vice, and by *Walker, Texas Ranger.*

I enjoy some shows and scorn others while sitting on my couch
repeating, "That's not the real world!" But it is authentic when riding
with *COPS* on the beat for the *Alaska State Troopers.* So whether I
bounce from *Hill Street Blues* to *The Profiler,* I applaud when criminal
conduct is uncovered in the *Dragnet* because the action is *Justified.*

As a youngster I wanted to *Get Smart* as *Adam 12* inspired me.
Eventually I became one of *The Rookies* hoping in time I would
make *S.W.A.T.* As my career progressed I donned a suit and became
Dick Tracy. Yet even interrogating crooks much like *The Closer,* I
often lamented that we could not solve crime with the speed of *CSI*
regardless of which city I was in.

I smiled with *Andy Griffith*, laughed at *Barney Miller*, and waited for *T.J. Hooker* to say, "Beam me up, Scotty." I had difficulty taking *Barnaby Jones* seriously as I waited for Jethro from another show to drop in and call him Uncle Jed.

That leads me to the telecasts involving P.I.'s which provided a certain level of amusement connected to law enforcement. The original *Charlie's Angels* captivated the attention of most teenage boys. Perhaps these lovely ladies inspired one or two young girls to become a real-life *Police Woman, Cagney and Lacey*, or something called *The Unusuals*.

Magnum P.I. promoted from civilian investigative work to become *The Commish* in *Blue Bloods*. Didn't we also see his alter ego as *Jesse Stone*, chief of police in the fictional town of Paradise, Massachusetts?

A good *Crime Story* solved by *The FBI* will make a *True Detective* tune in, while *Diagnoses Murder* never caught my *Eyes*. A few other shows gave me a desire to take a *Sledge Hammer* to the TV. *Murder, She Wrote* was one in particular; my apologies to those who enjoyed it.

Some who carried *The Shield* on camera defined what it meant to be cool, not corrupt. *Without a Trace* of timidity, *Baretta, Kojak,* and *The Mod Squad* displayed confidence in ways that made any *Police Story* entertaining.

McLoud along with *McMillan and Wife* were on a carousel of truth each Sunday night, but *Columbo* always had one more question before *Law and Order* was restored.

Car 54, Where Are You? They were found in the Bronx, while *Brooklyn Nine-Nine* is a different show altogether.

Geographically, *Vegas* is south of *Reno 911*, yet northeast of the highways patrolled by *CHiPs*.

Eclectically, *Starsky and Hutch* are as polar opposite as *NCIS* and *21 Jump Street*, yet they all succeeded as *True Blue* thrillers. *Hawaii Five-0* caught a wave in the late 60s and hit the surf again more than forty years later.

In real life, *Moonlighting* as *Simon and Simon* has been a strategy used by some cops to transition from sworn law enforcement to private investigative work. Others attend law school and *JAG* becomes reality.

Indeed, television has taken us from *LAPD: Life on the Beat* to *Ironside* solving *Major Crimes*. What's not to like about *Mannix* entertainment? It's all *In the Line of Duty*.

I'm not *Matlock* or *Perry Mason,* so I can't defend what I'm saying aloud, although I'm on *The Mentalist* for trying. But if I've been as smooth as *Matt Houston,* perhaps you'll find a place for *My Subtle Soliloquy* next to *The Rockford Files.*

All right you say mildly entertaining, but what's the point? A soliloquy is not a parable, and mine was written since you could not hear the oration. But there were portions you understood and others you did not. If I walked you through it line by line, the light might illuminate in areas that are presently mysterious. But there is no hidden meaning, it was simply used to amuse and then transition to a question worth answering. Why did Jesus often teach in parables?

"It was to conceal the truth 'for' us, not 'from' us," I once heard a pastor say. I believe he was on target based upon Matthew's testament when Jesus was asked the same question.

Then the disciples came and said to him, "Why do you speak to them in parables?" And he answered them, "To you it has been given to know the secrets of the kingdom of heaven, but to them it has not been given. For to the one who has, more will be given, and he will have an abundance, but from the one who has not, even what he has will be taken away. This is why

I speak to them in parables, because seeing they do not see, and hearing they do not hear, nor do they understand.[139]

Keep in mind, Jesus used parables when responding to questions by the Pharisees. Inquiries that were designed to box him into a corner. They thought they were quite clever when developing perceived *no-win* scenarios that would embarrass him. But each time Jesus demonstrated he was One with God, because his answers could not have been written any better by a brigade of wise advisors with nothing but time on their hands. One of my personal favorites is found in the book of Mark.

And he began to speak to them in parables. "A man planted a vineyard and put a fence around it and dug a pit for the winepress and built a tower, and leased it to tenants and went into another country. When the season came, he sent a servant to the tenants to get from them some of the fruit of the vineyard. And they took him and beat him and sent him away empty-handed. Again he sent to them another servant, and they struck him on the head and treated him shamefully. And he sent another, and him they killed. And so with many others: some they beat, and some they killed. He had still one other, a beloved son. Finally he sent him to them, saying, 'They will respect my son.' But those tenants said to one another, 'This is the heir. Come, let us kill him, and the inheritance will be ours.' And they took him and killed him and threw him out of the vineyard. What will the owner of the vineyard do? He will come and destroy the tenants and give the vineyard to others. Have you not read this Scripture:

"'The stone that the builders rejected

has become the cornerstone; this was the Lord's doing,

and it is marvelous in our eyes'?"

---

[139] Matthew 13:10–13

And they were seeking to arrest him but feared the people, for they perceived that he had told the parable against them. So they left him and went away.[140]

In the parable, the man is God. The vineyard represents Israel. The servants are the Old Testament prophets and John the Baptist. The son whom they killed is Jesus. The prediction of the destruction of the vine-growers was fulfilled when Jerusalem was destroyed in AD 70.[141]

As Jesus foretold of his own demise, he quoted from Psalm 118:22. Yet they did not get it, nor did they understand his standing as the prophesied Messiah.

The study Bible I used referred to them as *obdurate* religious leaders—stubbornly refusing to change their opinion or course of action.[142] Be mindful that *religion* is the attempt of humans to get to God. Jesus incarnate—God in the form of man—is God's plan to reach humanity. In the parable, Jesus admonished the *obdurate* ones who were unable to *see, hear,* or *understand.*

If you are wondering what to do with this message, pray and ask God to help you *see* his work in your life, *hear* the truth of his Word, and *understand* what his call to action is as you trust and obey.

Author's Note: There are sixty-eight television shows related to law enforcement named in this soliloquy. Here is the complete list:

---

[140] Mark 12:1–12

[141] Charles Caldwell Ryrie – Ryrie study Bible, *New American Standard Bible* (Chicago, Moody Press, 1977), 1528

[142] Ibid

Adam 12 – Alaska State Troopers – Baretta – Barnaby Jones – Barney Miller – Blue Bloods – Brooklyn Nine-Nine – Cagney and Lacey – Car 54, Where are You? – Charlie's Angels – Chicago P.D. – CHiPs – Columbo – COPS – Crime Story – CSI Las Vegas, Miami, NY – Dick Tracy – Dragnet – Get Smart – Hawaii Five-O – Hill Street Blues – Ironside – JAG – Jesse Stone – Justified – Kojak – LAPD Life on the Beat – Law and Order – Line of Duty – Magnum P.I. – Major Crimes – Mannix – Matlock – Matt Houston – McLoud – McMillan and Wife – Miami Vice – Moonlighting – NCIS – NYPD Blue – Perry Mason – Police Story – Police Woman – Reno 911 – Simon and Simon – Sledge Hammer – Southland – Starsky and Hutch – S.W.A.T. – The Andy Griffith Show – The Closer – The Commish – The FBI – The Mentalist – The Mod Squad – The Profiler – The Rockford Files – The Rookies – The Shield – The Streets of San Francisco – The Unusuals – T.J. Hooker – True Blue – True Detective – Vegas – Walker, Texas Ranger – Without a Trace – 21 Jump Street

SECTION TEN
DEBRIEFING

42

GOD'S 9-1-1 SYSTEM

*"To follow in God's shadow means
I need to walk toward the light."*

n previous chapters I've made references to Bible verses (Proverbs 10:19 and Psalm 10:15) with numerals synonymous to police radio code (10-19 – "at the station," and 10-15 – "suspect in custody") and used them as teaching points.

I have one more as we near the end of our journey. Naturally, we all know dialing 9-1-1 will get you to an emergency services dispatcher. Their duty is pretty crazy at times. They take the calls, send the officers, absorb the wrath, counsel the distraught, and instruct over the phone when life is in peril!

In their work center we dim the lights, skew the hue, for mental tranquility it's got to be blue! We've discovered that a soothing ambiance has a calming effect on the champions "behind the mic"— people who hear more tragic news per day than most will experience in a lifetime.

This group of professionals listen to words that sound like crank phone calls, but people on the other end of the line are actually serious. "I gotta bear in my pool! Get someone here quick!" hollers the one soliciting assistance on the emergency line. On the rare occasion there is a bear, but typically it's a large possum or other marsupial that is found.

"You better send someone fast, cuz' I'm about to shoot my man. He came home smelling like the cocktail waitress!" exclaims a distressed woman looking for help.

"Ma'am, please put the gun down and don't shoot your husband. We have officers on the way."

Dispatchers are required to translate *crazy* into *sane*, an acquired skill that takes time. *"Hurry, hurry, hurry!* It looks like an explosion on the street next to the all-night convenient store. Car parts and bodies everywhere!" shouts the reporting party.

"Units respond code three (lights and siren) to an injury collision at the corner of Fifth and Main," says the skilled dispatcher with a calm voice. "Fire/Rescue is en route."

The next call can be as diverse as a complaint about a broken water line that is flooding a local street, or the barbaric act of one human destroying another with a meat cleaver.

Dispatchers link citizens to the assistance they need, and officers to helpful resources while offering services to others. At times the dispatch center can be busier than Grand Central Station, and other moments as calm as a library. But there is always an assuring voice to answer 9-1-1 and capable of triaging the tragic tale being told so people receive the aid that is needed.

Divinely, a helpful verse to memorize and apply in time of need is Psalm 91:1, "He who dwells in the shelter of the Most High will abide in the shadow of the Almighty."

Using the *observe, reflect,* and *apply* method of studying Scripture, let's dissect this verse.

Observations

- ➤ "He (or she) who dwells…,"
  To remain, or take up residency!
- ➤ "…in the shelter…,"
  Something that provides protection from harm or the weather.
- ➤ "…of the Most High…,"
  God Almighty
- ➤ "…will abide…,"
  Submissive connection—grafted into that which is stronger, for strength and guidance.
- ➤ "…in the shadow…,"
  Following close behind.
- ➤ "…of the Almighty…."
  My Lord.

So my observations of this verse read like this. "I will remain a resident, protected from harm by God Almighty, and be submissively grafted for strength and guidance as I follow close to my Lord."

Reflections

- ➤ How do I take up residency?
  Say yes to God's invitation and begin a personal relationship with his Son, Jesus Christ.
- ➤ What does spiritual shelter look like?
  When viewing circumstances with an eternal perspective, nothing can harm me. My health and wealth can be lost in this world, but no one can take my hope in God's assurances, let alone damage my spirit or my soul.

> ➤ God Almighty is sovereign!
> This attribute gives him the ability to rule his creation while allowing me to experience free will.
> ➤ What does it mean to be grafted?
> Integral connectivity! I need to yield to his instruction so it permeates my thoughts and actions. I cannot be spiritually nourished if I pinch the source of supply.

Applications

> ➤ Residency compels me to affectionately spend time in God's Word and with the bride of Christ—the church.
> ➤ Acceptance to abide in his shadow is immediate, but yielding to his instruction to reinforce the grafting is a continual process.
> ➤ To follow in God's shadow means I need to walk toward the light.

You will have your own *observations, reflections,* and *applications* of this text—and I encourage you to do so. The Reformation Bible Commentary says it succinctly: "Those who draw near to God can have peace in him, however difficult their circumstances."[143] I believe you will find it easy to remember by simply referring to Psalm 91:1 as *God's 9-1-1 System.*

---

[143] https://www.biblegateway.com/resources/reformation-study-bible/Ps.91.1 – accessed on January 8, 2016.

TELL OPHIDIA TO TAKE A HIKE

43

"People head toward ruin because pride is valued more than truth."

The Golden Rule says, "So whatever you wish that others would do to you, do also to them...."[144] This well-known bit of instruction from Jesus motivates my next expression with a sense of urgency. God's perfect justice is a road less traveled even though it has been well marked in the best-selling book of all time—the Bible. I would like you to be on that boulevard with me.

Let me illustrate with a fictional story, *Justice Prevails in the End.* Here is the cast of characters to help you follow along:

Ignorant – A person before Christ was revealed to him
Illumination – A New follower of Christ – Formerly known as *Ignorant*
Fool – An unconverted person who rejects Christ
Ambiguous – An unconverted person who is confused about God
Robbed – It represents sin of every kind
Ophidia – A group of snakes representing Satan
Evil – An unconverted person heavily influenced by *Ophidia*

---

[144] Matthew 7:12

Microphone – A news reporter
Lamb – Jesus Christ
Power – The Holy Spirit
Justice – God the Father
Wisdom Patrol – The Body of Christ, the Church
Sword – The Word of God, the Bible

Justice Prevails in the End

Ignorant and *Fool* walked into a convenient store without realizing it was being *robbed*. Seeing that *Evil* had the drop on the clerk, self-preservation kicked in and *Ignorant* dove for cover while *Fool* stood in shock.

When *Evil* fled, the *Wisdom Patrol* responded. *Ophidia* successfully shielded *Fool* from seeing the truth so he could not provide anything useful. *Ignorant* accurately told what he'd seen. As *Ignorant* told his story, *Wisdom Patrol* shared the truth about *Evil* and the main conspirator behind all his activities, *Ophidia*.

Ignorant was interested in hearing more about the conflict between good and *Evil*, so the *Wisdom Patrol* told him about *Lamb, Power,* and *Justice.* The experience changed *Ignorant's* perspective on life. He discovered that *Lamb* is the only way to discover *Justice,* and *Power* was available as he surrendered his heart and mind to the truth of the good news found in the *Sword*. He embraced his new identity and became known as *Illumination,* and eventually joined the *Wisdom Patrol.*

Years later, *Illumination* approached the same convenient store. He remembered being *Ignorant*, so his new identity kicked in. *Illumination* looked through the front window before entering the market. *Evil* had returned and once again the employee was standing there with arms raised. Possessing compassion for the clerk and fellow patrons, *Illumination* drew knowledge obtained from the *Sword*, which tactically ended the showdown.

Later that week, *Fool* and his friend, *Ambiguous*, walked into another store being *robbed* by *Evil's* twin brother, who was unwittingly acting under the influence of *Ophidia*. After mumbling unintelligibly, *Fool* apologized to *Evil* for his plight while *Ambiguous* froze in his tracks, unable to move or speak. *Fool* implored the clerk and other patrons to surrender their possessions because *Evil* had the greater need. As *Evil* fled, he maliciously bulldozed a customer while yelling something about supremacy and power.

When *Illumination* and his on duty partners from *The Wisdom Patrol* arrived, *Fool* distorted the truth because he sympathized with *Evil*. *Ambiguous* accurately relayed a few facts, but his mind was still confused by all he'd seen. Regardless of his plight, he thanked *Wisdom Patrol* for the response.

Microphone from the local news arrived on scene and stuck a recording device in front of *Fool*. *Fool* denied his deception and asserted hope that *Evil* was brought to *Justice*.

Illumination knew *Justice* well as his life became brighter with instruction from *Lamb* and help from *Power*.

In prayer, *Illumination* asked for discernment and understanding when challenged by *Evil*, and befriending *Fool* and *Ambiguous* in the midst of trickery by *Ophidia*.

"No temptation has overtaken you that is not common to man," answered *Justice*. "I am faithful, and will not let you be tempted beyond your ability, but with the temptation I will also provide the way of escape, that you may be able to endure it."[145]

"Thank you, *Justice*," replied a grateful *Illumination*.

---

[145]   1 Corinthians 10:13

"I am the way, the truth, and the life. No one comes to the Father but through me,"[146] *Lamb* reminded *Illumination*. "And just as I told my disciples when I ascended into Heaven," *Lamb* continued, "I have sent *Power* as your helper. He will teach you all things and bring to your remembrance all that I have said to you."[147]

"Yes, *Lamb*," acknowledged a resolute *Illumination*. "I will remember as I remain armed with the *Sword* to counter illusions formed by *Ophidia*."

"Finally," declared *Justice*, "remain true to *Wisdom Patrol* and do not be discouraged by this *Fool* or any other. *Ophidia's* reign of terror is temporary. Be sure you resort to my *Sword* for answers, as other options distort the truth, thus developing one *Ambiguous* person after another."

Following the upheaval, *Illumination* sipped his morning coffee as he sat quietly on the patio reading from his *Sword*, "And this gospel of the kingdom will be proclaimed throughout the whole world as a testimony to all nations, and then the end will come."[148]

Through the teaching of *Lamb* along with help from *Power*, *Illumination* learned that *Justice Prevails in the End*.

Hopefully you detected the story was rife with symbolism. We have the *Ignorant, Ambiguous,* and *Fool(ish)* among us. In the real world outside of this story, we have all been *ignorant fools* being influenced by the *evil* prince of the world—Satan. Using *ambiguity*, he leads us to believe the path is wide, but it's deceptive.

The truth contained in Scripture is the gospel of Christ Jesus. He not only gave us the Golden Rule as mentioned earlier, directly following it he said, "Enter by the narrow gate. For the gate is wide and the way is easy that leads to destruction, and those who enter by

---

[146] John 14:6

[147] John 14:26

[148] Matthew 24:14

it are many. For the gate is narrow and the way is hard that leads to life, and those who find it are few."[149]

Matthew quotes Jesus, exhorting that we live by the Golden Rule, quickly followed by the reality of a "narrow gate."

I find it interesting that most people uniformly accept the Golden Rule, while teaching of the *narrow gate* is criticized and dismissed because those adverse to the Christian worldview claim it promotes intolerance.

If I invite everyone to a party at my house and tell those in attendance they need to enter through the front door because there are bloodthirsty dogs in the rear, is that intolerant or realistic? Is a traffic officer narrow-minded when telling a motorist to turn around when driving the wrong way on a one-way street? Is the young ensign assigned to a lighthouse incorrect when advising the captain of a warship to alter course to avoid a collision? The answer is a resounding no, no, no!

With respect and compassion for all, I would like to counsel that Satan has people facing vicious dogs, driving on the wrong side of the road, and vessels aimed at lighthouses. People head toward ruin because pride is valued more than truth.

"Submit yourselves therefore to God," wrote James, the brother of Jesus, "Resist the devil, and he will flee from you."[150] If I can make things simple, I would recommend saying yes to Jesus, and *Tell Ophidia to Take a Hike!*

---

[149] Matthew 7:13,14

[150] James 4:7

GRACIOUS REDEMPTION

44

Gracious Redemption has purified my heart, galvanized my soul, and solidified the Holy Spirit in my life.

I wrote the prose, "Gracious Redemption," while pouring out my heart to the Lord in prayer. It is filled with instruction from the greatest philosopher of all time, Jesus Christ, so you can be certain that concrete truth is present!

Gracious Redemption

Shame and regret pound my soul when I repeat what I hate. Then I'm reminded that I've been graciously redeemed. Living incomplete is cast aside.

Grace—God's riches at Christ's expense; commuted judgment for eternal blessing; unmerited favor with the Father.

Redemption—A debt that I cannot pay has been canceled, which leads to liberating reconciliation with God.

So *Gracious Redemption* is embraced, treasured, and valued more than my next breath. For there is a day when worldly breathing will cease and a Heavenly Father will ask, "What did you do with my Son?"

Believe and receive, that's what I did! I surrender. I hide no more.

Do I seek God or does he pursue me? The reality is that he's calling me as I hide,

just as a shepherd seeks a lost lamb.

Here I am, Lord. Thank you for finding me. When shame recurs because of this game of "hide and seek," thank you for *Gracious Redemption*!

Part of the deal includes *Justification*—Obtaining Christ's perfection, just as if I had never sinned. My name is written in the Lamb's Book of Life!

Unworthy describes my qualifications, but Jesus said, "I will confess his name before my Father, and before the angels."

Is there a better advocate?

I offer gratitude for justification!

May godliness prevail over my tendency toward ungodliness, or simply keeping my Lord safely tucked away on the shelf.

While shame is benched because God has called me to *Gracious Redemption*, I want it to fuel my desire to immerse in the Spirit of God; to run toward the light rather than injuring myself by hitting obstacles in dark places.

Here I am, Lord. Thank you for removing the veil, for revealing the truth that now saturates my soul. I surrender. Hiding from you might provide temporary pleasure, but the "pleasure train" *always* runs off track.

I offer thanksgiving for sanctification—you've set me aside for holiness.

In doing so, I submit my will to your way.

You are the potter, I am the clay

Since I want to serve you, I will follow.

As I follow, may I bring honor and glory to your name.

The filters that I use will be found in your Word

In faith I will see with your eyes, hear with your ears.

Gracious Redemption is real, authentic, and tangible.

Here I am Lord, imperfect, but I'm imperfectly yours.

Thank you that *Gracious Redemption* has purified my heart, galvanized my soul, and solidified the Holy Spirit in my life.

Here I am Lord, I am yours, use me!